EARLS HAVE PEACOCKS

EARLS
HAVE
PEACOCKS

THE MEMOIRS OF

Lord Howard de Walden

HAGGERSTON PRESS

© Lord Howard de Walden 1992

First published 1992
by the Haggerston Press
38 Kensington Place, London W8 7PR

Typeset by Fakenham Photosetting Ltd,
Fakenham, Norfolk
Printed in Great Britain
by Redwood Press Ltd, Melksham

1 869812 09 3

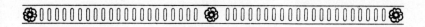

Contents

Illustrations

*I dedicate this book
to my eighteen grandchildren
and hope that they,
and perhaps a few others,
will find some amusement
in these pages*

Preface

THE ONLY REASONS I HAVE FOR WRITING THIS Preface are to thank those kind and helpful ladies, Mrs William Cundall and my secretary Mrs Crowe, who achieved the near-impossible by reading my handwriting, and to explain the title of this book. It came about in this way. Some years ago I was staying with the Earl of Scarborough at Sandbeck, his family home in Yorkshire. It was the 200th anniversary of the St Leger, run at Doncaster, and on the Sunday all the house party attended a service at the local church.

Dickon Scarborough and Liz, his wife, had asked a number of local dignitaries to have drinks before lunch. I was sitting in a car next to some very worthy lady as we drove through the gates into the Park. There were quite a number of pheasants about and this lady turned to me and said in broad Yorkshire, 'Eeh, what are they?' So I said, 'They are pheasants', to which she replied, 'Oh! I thought Earls had peacocks.' At once I said to myself, 'What a wonderful title for a book', and finding no other, I have stuck to it.

CHAPTER ONE

Meetings in Munich

THE SKY WAS REASONABLY CLEAR AND THE AIR warm in Munich on the 22nd of August, 1934. Quite early on the loudspeakers began to blare and the voice of Herr Goebbels explained once again why the beloved Führer had been obliged to kill Herr Roehm and a good many others, some six weeks earlier, on what became known as 'The Night of the Long Knives'. It was my wedding day and I was not concentrating very much on the propaganda as I lay in bed in the Hotel Continental. Equally, I felt no apprehension at what lay ahead. I was 21 years old and full of confidence, despite the fact that my marriage was highly unpopular with both my mother and father. Of course it was understandable that it should be so. I was the eldest and only son; that my wife-to-be was two years older than me didn't signify, but she was German, which signified a lot, and she was also a Roman Catholic, which signified a great deal more, especially as far as my mother was concerned.

It had been a long courtship, not such a rare thing in those days. After leaving Eton, I had been to Kenya for some months and was due to go to Spain to learn the language, as I had studied it for a short time at school. However, there was some trouble in Spain at the time and I was, therefore, despatched to Munich to stay with the Pappenheims and learn German instead; the year was 1931. Haupt Pappenheim, my host, was in his 60s, a small man with grey hair and a very extrovert manner, a real old-fashioned roué. On one occasion he had taken a fancy to a girl who worked in an office in the centre of town. I doubt whether he had even spoken to her, but so keen was he that he wrote his endearments on a blackboard and carried it above his head outside her window in the hope that she would respond. I hope she did. His wife was very large and very kind and seemed to put up with her husband's excesses, probably because he had always been like that.

When I had been there about a week, I bought myself a small car. I remember it with affection; it was a red Fiat and was very rudely referred to by my friends as the 'Commercial Traveller'. On my first day of driving I took Haupt Pappenheim with me so that I could learn the streets in the town and avoid being arrested for some misdemeanour. We drove slowly up the Luitpoldstrasse, past the Siegestor and up the Ludwigstrasse towards Odeonsplatz. All this area has been beautifully restored since the war and looks almost exactly the same as it did in those days. I took a right turn and although I was going very slowly, a man walked off the pavement, more or less straight into my car. He went down on one knee, but he was soon up and I knew that he wasn't hurt. I opened the window and naturally, as I hadn't a word of German, let Haupt Pappenheim do the talking. I was more anxious about whether a policeman, who was directing the traffic, had seen the incident. As soon as all was well, and we had shaken hands and driven on, Haupt Pappenheim said, 'I don't suppose you know who that was?' 'Of course I don't, who is he?' I replied. 'Well, he is a politician with a party and he talks a lot, his name is Adolf Hitler.' So, for a few seconds perhaps, I held the history of Europe in my rather clumsy hands.

I was later taken by my host to hear Hitler speaking and in 1934, when he had been Chancellor for about a year, I found myself sitting in the next box to him at the opera, in that charming little rococo theatre, which in those days was called the Residenz Theater. It was fortunately saved from destruction and is now known as the Cuvillié Theater. My moment had arrived and, leaning across, to the dismay of some black-shirted aides I asked the Führer if he remembered the incident. To my surprise he did and was quite charming to me for a few moments. We never met again.

I was in Munich for about three months in 1931 and had it not been for two friends who were there at the same time, my whole life would have taken another turn. Oswald Mulgrave (now the Marquess of Normanby) was staying with a family called Harrach, in Biedersteinerstrasse, and when we met one day he said to me, 'You ought to come and meet my people. Why don't you and Gerald come and have a swim in the pool tomorrow?' Gerald Cuthbert was a most attractive person, sadly killed a few years before the war. Gerald and I, for some strange reason, got rather tight that evening and thought it would be very funny to buy a big fish and surreptitiously put it in the Harrach pool. Pool is perhaps a bit of a misnomer; it was round and only about fifteen feet across, and would not be considered for swimming now, nor was it seriously then.

We bought the fish in the market and transported it in a large wooden container. Climbing the wall into the garden in the early hours unseen, we deposited the fish in the pool and returned for our swims some time later, looking very innocent. Quite a number of the family and friends were there, but not curiously enough Nucci, the youngest daughter, who later was to become my wife. As the water was rather murky and our friend was swimming slowly round at the bottom, nothing transpired until my future sister-in-law, Cucca, ventured in and found her ankles being tickled by an unknown monster. My Mother-in-law thought the whole thing was a huge joke and was quite convinced that some eccentric friend of the family had perpetrated it. As we were about to leave, Gerald and I felt that we had better own up. Our confession was met with astonishment, but it was insisted that we should return on the next day for lunch and eat the fish. Without this piece of foolishness I would never have met Nucci, who was there the next day. I fell in love at first sight and was even imprudent enough to write to my Mother to say that I had seen the girl that I intended one day to marry. I was 18 at the time. My Mother carefully kept the letter with the object of teasing me in years to come. I hope sincerely that I refrained from saying, 'I told you so', three years later.

I went to Cambridge in the Autumn of 1931 and throughout my three years there I visited Munich as often as possible. The journey was quite a difficult business in those days. Probably the easiest and the quickest way was to catch an aeroplane from Croydon in the morning. These very curious machines were named after cities, carried about sixteen passengers and took four hours to Cologne, which was as far as you could go. One spent the afternoon in that town and caught the night train to Munich, arriving early the next morning: twenty-four hours instead of approximately two hours today. The return was similar. On one occasion I was booking my ticket to return at the travel office in Promenadeplatz, when Nucci said, 'Oh, why don't you stay another day and go on the Orient Express instead?' Although I demurred, because it entailed changing my tickets and plans, she was so insistent that I finally gave in. When I arrived two mornings later on the Orient Express in Paris, on its way to Calais, I bought a newspaper and was horrified to see the headline, 'CITY OF LIVERPOOL CRASHES, ALL FIFTEEN KILLED'. I was the sixteenth who did not fly that day. The body of one of the passengers was found with an unopened parachute a little way from the rest of the debris, and he was apparently wanted by the police. Whether he sabotaged the plane and hoped to get away, will never be known.

After the initial shock I suddenly realised that my parents would think that I was dead, since I had failed to tell them of my change of plan, so I got off the train and went to the nearest hotel to telephone, in those days quite a performance. However, the phone was eventually answered by our large, friendly and fat hall porter called Davis. It took me some moments to persuade him that I was no ghost and ask him to inform my parents that all was well and that they need not buy any crepe. Incidentally, many years later Nucci stopped us both going to Ireland on a plane which crashed, killing about a hundred people. These were the only two presentiments that she had, or the only ones that I remember.

The other way to go to Munich, which I used more and more, was to drive. One took a ferry across to Calais or to Boulogne, in the morning, and then drove on to Nancy, where I used to stay the night in the beautiful Place Stanislas. The next morning I would go on via Lunéville across the border at Appenweier and up the winding road to Tübingen, then on to Munich by about teatime. I had two alarming experiences on that drive. On one occasion, after crossing the border and before climbing to Tübingen, there seemed to be a lot of people about including a number of Nazis, all waving and also trying to stop me. I paid no attention and, in my smart Alvis Speed 20 with three carburettors, roared up the road. There were people all the way and I suddenly realised that I was in some sort of motor race. So much so that, when I arrived sweating in Tübingen, someone rushed out with a checkered flag. I did not remain to receive the trophy! On the second occasion I thought I would try and take a different route. I got lost and found myself driving into a large forest. I was immediately arrested as I was in the midst of an army gathering with many tanks, etc, but I was released fairly quickly. On my return to England, when I told my friends about it, and particularly my father's friends, they laughed and said the tanks were all made of papier mâché. I was in the Territorials and knew a tank when I saw one. Neither the great French army nor the brass hats in ours believed reports of such sightings either, as we all learnt to our cost in the years to come. For myself, as I saw the rise of the Nazis I gradually became aware that something very nasty was going to happen in the not-too-distant future.

Nucci and I had been privately engaged for at least three years and we never had any illusions about it. I think I was influenced by some of the books and novels I had read concerning couples in the previous war with relations and friends on both sides. My Mother-in-law was one of the few people who had the courage to say exactly what she thought and even to upbraid the Nazi Stormtroopers when they were breaking the fronts of Jewish shops. She was also seen tearing down the more outrageous propaganda posters off the trees and buildings in the Ludwigstrasse and elsewhere. Why she was not arrested I shall never know, probably because she appeared highly eccentric and rather old, although she was only about 60 at the time.

Of course, there were all the pleasant things to enjoy as well. Being a newcomer to opera, I endeavoured to give myself indigestion by attending twenty-one different performances in as many days. I used to get very excited if I thought the performance of say, *The Marriage of Figaro*, was better in Munich than in Salzburg and I used to force my friends attending the Salzburg Festival to come and see and hear for themselves. I still think that Heinrich Rehkemper was wonderful in *Figaro* and *Don Giovanni* and Julius Patzak's lyric tenor was something no one will forget who heard him in his heyday. I can also remember with great affection Felicie Hüni-Mihachek as the Countess in *Figaro*. The little restaurants that we used to visit were charming: one in particular, where the small band played 'Parlez Moi d'Amour' whenever we came in.

The evening before a wedding in Germany there is a *Polterabend*, or formal reception, and ours took place at Nucci's home. One or two people who were expected did not turn up and for the first time I heard the whisper, 'he's been taken to Dachau'. Of course this was only one year after the Nazis came to power and presumably the concentration camps were positively benign compared to their future nauseating history. However, it was alarming and there was no communication with those taken nor any redress. Haupt Pappenheim, now an even older roué, distinguished himself by coming in a Luftwaffe uniform with a Nazi emblem on his arm. This was not greeted with any enthusiasm and I am sure it was his last visit to that house. Actually, I suspect it was also his first.

My family, although far from enthusiastic, all came to my wedding except, sadly, my twin sister Bronwen, who had only just given birth to her first son, Hugh. The day before, we had to attend a civil ceremony with the English Consul present which, as things turned out, was extremely lucky. When the War was over, I had, for some reason, to produce my marriage certificate, only to find that all these records had been destroyed by our bombers. Fortunately, the British Foreign Office was able to vouch that all had been carried out correctly. Sadly, I have lost the book given by the Hitler regime to newly married couples; I have no recollection that we either studied or even red its homilies!

All my other four sisters were bridesmaids, together with Cucca, Nucci's sister, and other friends. The wedding itself was charming and the small church, Dreifaltigkeitskirche, still stands at the entrance to Promenadeplatz. We were married in the morning and afterwards had a lovely family lunch in Biedersteinerstrasse, at which I remember only the course 'Krebschwänze auf eine Besondere Art': crayfish in dill sauce. The lunch was prepared by the famous Walterspiel whose restaurant, then attached to the Hotel Vier Jahreszeiten, was world-renowned. We were to spend the first night of our honeymoon at the Insel Hotel on Lake Constance. It was quite a long drive and once again we set off in the faithful Alvis. I do remember feeling a little dazed, probably by the excellent wine, and stopping to put my head under a small stream gushing out of the side of a hill. We arrived in the dark, very tired, hoping as so many others before and after us that no one would notice we were covered with both confusion and confetti. There was one guest dressed in the inevitable uniform sitting in the hall to watch our arrival; I knew his face and still do. His name was Rudolph Hess.

Nucci's father's family, the Harrachs, came from Vienna; their picture collection is world-famous. One of the Harrach Ladies had married the Emperor Frederick of Prussia, as his second wife. Owing to the political tensions at the time, the Emperor had found it rather embarrassing to have a brother-in-law in the Austrian army. He had therefore suggested to him that if he came and settled in Prussia and became a Protestant he, the Emperor, would see that he had a nice estate. As the young man was not the head of his family, there was no reason why he should not better himself in this way and he accepted this suggestion. The estate was at Tiefhartsmandorf and there he raised a family. The fine house has long since been destroyed by the Russians.

My father-in-law took up painting, following his father who had been a painter but later became a sculptor. When he got engaged to a beautiful Bavarian lady, Helene Arco Zinneberg, and married her, he was disinherited because she was a Catholic. I am glad that my parents took a rather more lenient view when I got married. My father-in-law moved with his new wife to Florence, where they lived until the outbreak of war in 1914. Whilst my father-in-law joined his regiment, the family were settled in Switzerland at the glorious Castle of Oberhofen, which belonged to the Pourtalès family, Nucci's grandmother's.

It was to see this castle, where Nucci was brought up during those war years, that we repaired on leaving Rudolph Hess at the Insel Hotel on Lake Constance. My father-in-law and his mother had sold the castle after the war to an American and with the money, or at least part of it, built their house, No. 21a Biedersteinerstrasse, in Munich. As this was the period of really crazy inflation, it was certainly the wisest and best thing that could have happened. Otherwise what little money there was, would have vanished, or rather the banknotes would have become wall decorations, as I even can remember as a child.

We stayed at a charming little pension on a hill above the castle which is on the edge of, and partly built out into, the lake, the Thunersee. When the young porter, with his smart green apron, carried our luggage up to our bedroom, he opened the windows wide and started to give a historical dissertation about the castle lying beneath us. After a short while Nucci interrupted him and in her best Swiss said, 'You don't seem to remember me, we sat next to each other at school'. After that, nothing was too much trouble. We were shown round the castle by the American owner and were a little surprised to find photographs of us both in a number of rooms. We began to wonder if he was considering leaving the castle back to Nucci as a member of the family. Whatever thoughts may have been in his mind, he did in fact leave it to the Swiss State, a very reasonable solution.

Honeymoons are not for writing about. We were going to Italy and all that need be said is that many of the passes were already blocked, which was surprising for late August, and it rained wherever we went. I remember two nights on straw mattresses in attics, and also returning to our bedroom after dinner in an hotel on Lake Garda and finding the room aswarm with bats. I shall never forget either the word 'Pipistrelli' or the wild way the staff dealt with them, breaking at least two mirrors and several light bulbs. The blocking of the WC with moribund bats meant a change of room for us.

After Vienna we returned to London via Paris, where my mother was staying at the time. We were hoping that we would be given lovely meals we could not afford, but no, my mother took the very tiresome view that the 'young things' should be left alone. I had chosen a little house in John Street, now Chesterfield Hill, in Mayfair, as a temporary home while we looked for something more permanent. I started work in the City with a firm of stockbrokers and Nucci was left to fend for herself in a town she didn't know, in a language in which she was not perfect and with no help from the family at all. Before my wedding my mother had told my sisters, who in those days were as putty in her hands, that they were not to be nice to Nucci, as she didn't wish her to marry me. They seemed to continue the attitude when the reason was no longer there.

My first effort at employing domestic staff was not auspicious. I had taken over a young footman called Leonard, who had a slight defect in his speech. He used to look after us as children in the schoolroom and, as his speech would presumably impair the likelihood of his advancing in his chosen profession, it was felt proper that he should come to us. Shortly afterwards a friend of mine, William Rhodes-Moorhouse, rang me up and asked me to go and see him. Apparently Leonard had lost all his money gambling and in despair had gone to William, who paid up. I gave Leonard a severe talking-to on the subject of greyhound racing and gambling in general, paid his debts and hoped for the best. However, the same thing soon happened again, so we decided to pay off Leonard once more and suggest that he had better face life without us. I hope that he learnt his lesson but, from the many other occasions I have had to deal with gamblers, I take leave to doubt it. The trouble about being a gambling addict is that, unlike an alcoholic, you don't feel awful in the morning.

In due course we found a nice house in Chapel Street, across the way from my parents in Belgrave Square, the second of the many and varied houses we were to live in. The following August our first child Hazel was born. She took a very long time to arrive and my father-in-law, with considerable thoughtfulness, sent me a telegram saying, 'Do not worry, elephants and Arcos take eleven months'. He was nearly right, and on each subsequent occasion the same thing happened.

CHAPTER TWO
My Father

IT SEEMS, PERHAPS, A STRANGE AND UNNECES-
sary thing to go prowling back into the recesses of the
past and to lift the decent curtain of death which has
covered the weary, ugly follies there. But I have just that
tempered belief in heredity which makes me think the
past will bear watching, lest certain devils that may be
lying in wait in our frames take us altogether unawares.
For it is only the unknown that is dangerous, especially in
one's own heart. Know your native devil and you can
laugh at him.

It was re-reading these words, taken from the long 'letter'
written to his son from Gallipoli and French campaigns in the
First World War, that has persuaded me to write about my
father. Perhaps it will be of interest to his descendants to know
what sort of man he was and, perhaps, to recognise in themselves some of his traits. Some fifty years after his death the
personality and the memories are a little faded. It is not my
intention to write a life of my father – he would have made
some very sarcastic remark if he thought I would dare such an
enterprise. However, in every generation a few men leave their
mark on their friends and relations that is indelible, despite the
fact that they accomplished no great worldly success and
played a very small part, if any at all, in the public life of their
country. My father was such a one. I do not think it is difficult
to understand the reasons for this, for he possessed several
ingredients, good and bad, that divided him from the ordinary.

23

These ingredients are fairly obvious if one reads the titles of his collected works and notes the great variety of subject matter. Anyone who was privileged to have heard his conversation must be sad that no tape recorder was there to preserve the mixture of love, chivalry and scorn that was allowed to flow over, mostly during the late hours of the night. He would speak with some authority on almost any subject one cared to mention, and his memory was prodigious. He was not gregarious and, indeed, was extremely shy. His views and opinions were his own; he had a great contempt for following the common herd and despised the follies of the political party system in particular. He called himself a miserable Jack of all Trades, but equally he could have thought of himself, how I think of him, as a fully rounded man.

He was a poet who was a fencer of international class with either hand; a thinker who could inspire many very intelligent young men to seek a way towards a better society and write witty children's pantomimes at the same time; a man of great wealth with several large homes who spent most of his happier moments painting in a little mews studio; a man who believed in the barbarian virtues of courage, courtesy and kindliness, and could be more devastatingly sarcastic than most; a first-class fisherman who could write a trilogy of Byzantine plays praised by the acknowledged authority on that little-known period; a man whose knowledge and interest in the breeding of racehorses was immense and whose favourite men were Kipling and Chesterton. One could go on endlessly.

Thomas Evelyn Ellis was born on the 9th May 1880, the first and only child of Frederick Ellis (The 7th Lord Howard de Walden) and Blanche Holden, eldest daughter of a good Lancashire family. Frederick was 50 years old at the time my father was born. It is necessary to go back to Frederick's parents to understand the strange behaviour of his family that was to form my father's background. Frederick's father,

Charles Augustus, was born in 1799 and became Lord Howard de Walden in 1803, succeeding his great-grandfather Frederick Augustus Hervey, the famous Bishop of Derry and 4th Earl of Bristol. Charles's life was a conventional one: some early years in the Army and then a career in the Foreign Service. He made his name during his years as Minister in Lisbon, when there was the civil war between the Miguelites and the Pedronites. The Queen of Portugal trusted him and his influence was very great. Afterwards he served for twenty-two years in Brussels and died in that country. In 1828 he had married Lady Lucy Cavendish-Bentinck, a daughter of the 4th Duke of Portland. On Lucy was settled a life interest in some Marylebone property with remainder to her son. This property, now known as the Howard de Walden Estate, was the source of her wealth.

There is a story that Lucy, a woman of great character, had her husband buried in a pauper's grave in Brussels on his death in 1868, and that her eldest son Frederick was so incensed at this that he never again spoke to his mother. Whether this be true or not, the fact is that he hated his mother, and no doubt the feeling was largely reciprocated. The result was that Frederick had little or no money, and as Lucy lived on until 1899, Frederick and Blanche's child Tommy (my father) was brought up with none of the background of that wealth which he was destined to inherit.

My father once said to me that he thought he had been conceived in spite, and I do not think this is greatly exaggerated. Frederick was a bachelor till the age of 46. He was a soldier by profession. He drank to excess and frequently disappeared for months and even years at a time. It would be natural for his brothers and cousins to have thoughts of inheriting the riches of Lucy, and Frederick's hatred of his mother would surely have encouraged him to thwart these hopes. Certainly the Holden family and many friends brought great pressure to bear on Blanche to persuade her not to marry this hard-drinking man. When eventually Blanche gave birth to a son, Frederick's reaction was typical of the man. He came and looked at the child and saw that he was a boy and healthy, then with hardly a word spoken he left the house, not to return or be seen for months to come.

Tommy, therefore, was brought up with few toys and spent a lot of time alone or with his Swiss nurse until he was sent to his preparatory school at Cheam. This was an unmitigated disaster, as the school at that time was in the charge of a man totally unsuited to look after children. He was sadistic and made the life of all the boys a hell. These facts were corroborated by many people later who had either been co-sufferers or even masters for a short time. This can hardly have been a happy influence on a shy, intelligent and rather introspective boy, but may have taught him the usefulness of the art of self-defence which he always considered to be the prerequisite of every gentleman.

By the time he went to Eton his parents were to all intents and purposes separated and he spent the greater part of his holidays with his mother. I think it is clear that the situation was not approved of by the Cavendish-Bentincks, as many of his holidays were spent at Welbeck and his education paid for, in fact, by the then Duke of Portland, a cousin of his grandmother Lucy.

Although my father cared for Eton almost as little as for Cheam, he did make a few friends who remained devoted all his life. He was shy and rather unpopular, very largely due to not liking the gregariousness then almost necessary to be a success at a British public school. Yet his two best friends, then and always, were Harry Morritt of Rokeby and Bobby Oppenheim, both essentially extrovert by nature. Harry was a magnificent fisherman and was good at all sports, as well as having a love and talent for painting. Bobby Oppenheim was half Jew, half Irish, and a man of great charm. He enjoyed the social life and drifted gently amongst his friends, loved by all, one of the real clubmen of London, conventional, kind and a delightful guest. Both these men were the antithesis of my father and yet both loved him all their lives, and one can say almost venerated him.

It was during these school years that he made friends with Mark Sykes, the son of Sir Tatton Sykes of Sledmere. Mark Sykes, as students of the period will know, was a man of great talent and gifts, and it is understandable that these two unconventional children should have drifted towards each other. During these years, two of the most celebrated studs in England were at Welbeck and Sledmere, and it can hardly be coincidental that in later years one of my father's hobbies and interests was the breeding of racehorses.

My father was short-sighted and always wore spectacles. Despite this handicap, it was considered that he would do better in an Army class at Eton, perhaps because there was more discipline in this class. He duly passed the examinations for Sandhurst and appeared for the medical. My father always said that the oculist's tests were done in an old-fashioned London pea-soup fog and, as no one could see anything, everybody was passed. How true this is I cannot guess, but something of the sort must have happened, as no one with eyes as bad as my father's could have passed into the Army under normal circumstances.

So there arrived at Sandhurst an intelligent, quiet, well-read young man with bad eyesight and few friends, but an interest in everything and a memory that was to be his greatest asset in life. I think he quite enjoyed Sandhurst or, rather, very little time was available for disliking it. It was decided that he should join the 10th Hussars and no doubt he expected a few years of peacetime soldiering as a young officer. But on 29th July 1899, his grandmother Lucy died and his father Frederick inherited the properties and family fortune. In October, the Boer War started and Tommy sailed to join his regiment at Cape Town; and on the 3rd November of the same year,

Frederick himself died. Frederick's last words to my father when he went to see him, both knowing that they would not meet again, were, 'Don't marry a fool'. As he himself said, 'This is good advice, but not all-embracing!'

He appears to have had no particular interest in his inheritance. His letters home to his mother are what one might expect. There are long complaints about Cape Town and the people and the boredom, and hopes of chocolate by the next mail. He was, like many other young men, highly critical of the Generals and considered the campaign was waged with extreme inefficiency. There was, however, invariably a humorous twist to his remarks and the poem to his commanding officer is typical of his lighter style. He was invalided back to England with malaria in February 1901, having been abroad for fourteen months. He resigned his commission in the 10th Hussars in the same year and joined the 2nd Company of the London Yeomanry as a Captain.

Now began the ten most fruitful years of his life. During this period he laid the foundation of his knowledge by intensive reading; he wrote the *Cauldron of Annwyn* based on the *Mabinogion*, *Lanval* set in his beloved medieval period, *Tamlane*, and a good deal of poetry. He also wrote the Byzantine plays: *Constans II*, *Justinian II* and *Heraclius*. This very abstruse and difficult period my father absorbed pretty well. I sent the plays to Sir Steven Runciman, the acknowledged expert on this period, who spoke very well of them and was interested in my father's ideas even if they were not quite the same as his! *Lanval* and *Tamlane* were about Merlin; Tamlane was the son of the Earl of Moray.

The three parts of *The Cauldron of Annwyn* were set to music by Josef Holebrooke and they were produced: – the *Children of Don* at the London Opera House by Oscar Hammerstein; *Dylan* by Sir Thomas Beecham and conducted by his son, Sir Thomas, at Covent Garden; and *Bronwen* in Liverpool by the Carl Rosa company. Of the Byzantine plays, to the best of my knowledge only *Heraclius* was produced, at the Festival Theatre in Cambridge.

He took a great interest in all literary matters. He became friendly with Bernard Shaw, G. K. Chesterton, Hilaire Belloc, Max Beerbohm and George Moore. He used his money to put on those plays that he thought ought to be seen. At one time he owned the Haymarket Theatre where he put on Ibsen's *Pretenders* and many other large-scale productions. It was typical of him that on one occasion he was told he was losing so much that the manager wished to close the theatre. He said, 'No, find something to fill the gap until I decide what to do.' Thereupon a small comedy was found called *Bunty Pulls the Strings*, which ran for two or three years and recouped all his losses. He never went to see it. He was greatly interested in music and helped support many orchestras; also in painting, and numbered Augustus John and Wilson Steer among his friends.

Apart from what we might call these intellectual pursuits, he had many other interests in which he indulged and in some of which he became expert. First in this category must come fencing. He took this up with enormous enthusiasm and although a late starter, he became extremely skilled with both hands, certainly up to international class. He was, in fact, the spare man in our Olympic team at Athens in 1908. He collected a library of rare books on the subject and became in time the authority who was consulted by everyone interested, both in his own country and abroad. It is hardly surprising that this should have led to his collecting both swords and armour, which are now housed in the Keep of Dean Castle at Kilmarnock, restored by him in detail from a total ruin.

Dean Castle was originally the home of the Boyd family and came into our family through the Scotts – my great-great-grandmother Henrietta married General Scott and her sister was married to the Duke of Portland. When my father inherited, the Ayrshire property was divided between himself and the Portlands and I remember him telling me of the awful muddles when he had a farm in their property and vice versa. My sister Bronwen and I were sent to the Dean during the First War, presumably for safety reasons. When my father restored the castle he went to infinite lengths to ensure that even the plaster ceiling came from another Scottish house – presumably destroyed – and so everything was correct and authentic.

Horse racing had fascinated him since his holidays at Welbeck and Sledmere and on the death of Major McCalmont in 1901 he bought his stable, lock, stock and barrel. He had very considerable success as an owner and breeder; though his interest never flagged, his lack of attention to detail was to lead to a deterioration because new blood was not introduced into his stud, and later his equine families went downhill.

He was intensely interested in things mechanical, which seldom was the case in men educated in the Cavalry in those days. He learnt navigation on a trip to South America and was a pioneer of the early speed boats, as well as the owner of several large yachts in which he spent a good deal of time, including taking a part of the Olympic team to Athens in 1908. He developed a passion for model boats – full working models – and spent a great deal of time building these and harbours for them on the lake at Chirk, in what became known as 'His Lordship's Nursery'. No doubt modern psychologists would say that this was compensation for having few toys as a child, and in his case I think it likely that they would be right. He had a pronounced leaning towards all things appertaining to the age of chivalry, so it is not surprising to find him taking up the sport of hawking. Until the outbreak of the Second World War he employed a falconer and delighted in the work of the birds, both in the flat Newmarket area and, in later years, on the moors in North Wales. Such were his main interests, together with commanding the 2nd Company of the London Yeomanry and fully enjoying the annual camp and week-ends spent with the regiment.

Against what background was this full life led? As soon as my father realised that he was now a very rich man, he set about using his money to do things or to get things done that otherwise would not have been possible. It is clear that at first he was anxious to give his mother the home he would have liked her to have had earlier. He bought 37 Belgrave Square, which was known as Sefton House, and renamed it Seaford House. It is now the Royal College of Defence Studies and a very large house indeed, best known for a magnificent marble staircase and hall that was put in by my father. I have heard it said – but can find no one who knows – that he bought the whole mine so as to get this beautiful coloured marble. His own bedroom there was decorated in the most simple medieval manner with appropriate small windows and a large sword hanging point downwards above the bed.

At the same time an interest in the family antecedents made him take Audley End near Saffron Walden on lease from Lord Braybrooke. This beautiful house, built originally by the first Lord Howard de Walden, was his home until 1911. Although he enjoyed the excellent shooting and the entertaining of friends in this house, he never liked it and he and they were made aware of an unpleasant atmosphere, so much so that they were afraid to go to bed. It is supposedly haunted, as it is built on the site of a monastery destroyed in the 16th century. In 1911 he became infatuated with Chirk Castle, the Welsh border home of the Myddeltons. He took a lease of this very large place with the object of later buying it. The castle was in a state of semi-ruin and over the years it was restored to a home of great comfort. Why he never bought it I do not know. It was probably due to both the advent of the Great War and also the difficulty of agreeing a price. I don't believe there was much discussion of price, as my father once told me that the Myddeltons had asked a million, which seems improbable for those days, and that was the end of the negotiations. It did not seem to worry him that he lived all his life and came to love every inch of somewhere that was not his. Over and above these houses there was his large yacht in which he cruised extensively in the Mediterranean.

Although he had no gambling instincts, he enjoyed the rather strange figures that flitted across the scene in Monte Carlo and other places on the Riviera. He often regaled me with stories of characters such as La Belle Otero and Basil Zaharoff, who was supposed to have financed all the wars of the time. I can remember my father telling me that he was actually present in the Casino when, at the main roulette table, red came up twenty-two times running followed by black twenty-four times. This is incredible and I hope there are records of this event; it must have ruined a lot of people. Those were the days when, if some person went into the garden and shot themselves, some Casino official would creep out and surreptitiously fill their pockets with money so that there could be no suggestion that the wretched person had committed suicide because of gambling.

La Belle Otero had a great rival at the time, whose name sadly escapes me, but every night these two ladies would parade through the Casino, each outdoing the other with more spectacular jewellery – until one evening the first lady appeared as usual dressed in everything. La Belle Otero followed in a plain black dress with her maid carrying all her jewellery on a cushion behind her. The result of this was a most unseemly scuffle when even hatpins came into play.

It is difficult at the present time and for our generation to visualise how each day was spent and how someone managed to do so many things in such a short period. However, if one can put away any thought of going to an office or even of writing letters except personal ones, there are many hours in each day, if they are usefully employed. An active mind and a voracious reader, who had no money worries, he had all day and long hours of the night in which to indulge in his sports and intellectual pursuits. My father did not by nature or by desire belong to the Edwardian society who seem to have been so busy in visiting each other's houses to shoot each other's pheasants and grouse, to change clothes several times a day and eat gargantuan meals. This is not to say that he didn't enjoy shooting but, after a surfeit at Welbeck and other houses, he gave it up for many years because he got bored. He was, in fact, a good shot and in later years took great enjoyment in the high birds that were the hallmark of the shoot at Chirk. He never went in for big bags and was only interested in the quality.

And so we find him during these ten years doing up Seaford House – starting the restoration of Dean Castle, Kilmarnock – living at Audley End – racing on a large scale – fencing every day of his life – hawking. Simultaneously he was discussing every interesting subject with the intelligent people of the period – running a theatre – financing orchestras and helping artists of all kinds – collecting armour and swords. He also managed to lose a large sum of money by backing enterprises in South America and Tanganyika that were doomed to failure by the charm but innate waywardness of their promoters.

The years slipped by and most of his friends and the world in which he moved thought of him as a confirmed bachelor. It would be unseemly for a son to discuss a father's attitude to women; in any case it is impossible for me to do so as I don't know what his was. That he was susceptible to ladies is certain and he always admitted it, but I venture to believe that what affairs he may have had at this time were neither serious nor long-lived. He had no Victorian reticence or puritan outlook on this matter. He often spoke about the disaster of the disappearing demi-mondaine. It was his contention – and it is difficult to refute – that these ladies, and ladies in the old-fashioned sense they were, did contribute to the style of the period as well as to a civilised education of the young gentleman in sex matters. My father could not see, and nor can I for that matter, that things have been improved by either the cold, efficient call-girl systems or the amateur stepping out of her background on unfamiliar territory for her own curiosity and gratification. However, these are all things of the past and each age has its own attitudes, good and bad.

As to his attitude to marriage, two things seem to stand out from his own writings. Firstly there is his consciousness of strange blood – 'Our family history has been compared to that of the Pougon Macqhart family.' He then goes on to say that he doubts whether anybody still reads Zola, and I think he was right. The second observation is that in the whole of his 'letter to his son' there is not one mention of his wife or women in general. He had been married for less than four years at the time. I do not propose to propound any great theory based on these facts, but merely to record that my father thought it advisable to marry right away from his own breeding: in other words, what would be called an 'outcross' in other species. This, I believe, can give 'hybrid vigour'. Whether the results of this union were what he hoped for or not I have no idea, but I would hazard a guess that he was disappointed. After all, most parents are.

When the war came in August 1914, my father did not greet it with the enthusiasm that was so prevalent at that time. His thinking about and knowledge of the weaknesses inherent in our political system had already made him anxious for the future. He felt a cloud of enormous proportions was hanging over the country and that it would need time and great endurance to overcome the trials that lay ahead. All these feelings are inherent in his writings, especially in the lovely preface to the *Cauldron of Annwyn* written in 1910 or 1911, which ends,

There is a word yet to be said about the mood of that in valediction. This work was written under the shadow of a gross impending storm. That storm has broken and is past but the seed of it will not die upon our shores whilst we are amongst the living. I am ashamed for a great deal of thought that is anxious and almost despairing. I tried to invent a primeval folk with faith because I had none. But having seen something of the valour innate and the proud, humourous spirit of our days, I grow still more ashamed.

For though new streams set in over the broken land and all our shores are strange; though the dynasties are gone and honour seems lost under the queer jetsam of these tides; yet Nodens dream on. [Nodens are mythical Welsh birds.]

He left with his regiment for Egypt in September 1914. He was attached the next year to the 29th Division for the Gallipoli expedition and was successively Military Landing Officer at Imbros and at Sulva Bay, and later Deputy Assistant Adjutant and Y.M.G. 29th Division. He was on the evacuation staff at Sulva in December 1915 and was one of the last people to leave after that sad and unhappy campaign. It is as well to remember that the expectation of life was no more than a few weeks for junior officers, when he was writing the letter to his son. I have been told stories of his sitting on a heap of ammunition under shell fire, apparently quite oblivious to any danger. That he was a brave man there can be no doubt, and it was courage that he admired most of the virtues. After Gallipoli he rejoined his regiment at El Daboa and in May 1916 went on leave to England, then in November became Second-in-Command of the 9th Battalion of the Royal Welch Fusiliers in France. He was with them until recalled to the War Office in December 1917.

These flat details are given simply to show that he had a very common war with no shirking of the unpleasant duties and no safe billet away from the firing line. His second daughter, Elizabeth, was born in December 1914 and the telegram he sent on learning the news always struck me as embodying a lot of his curious apparent lack of feeling. It read, 'Sorry Elisabeth' signed Howard. His views on girls were rather old-fashioned, as is exemplified in an extract from a letter to his cousin Stephen Powles in Kenya sometime during the Second War: 'Bronwen's eldest (Hugh) is a very bright lad. He is a mathematician of no mean order (where does he get it from?) and up to the standard of fourteen at ten years. The girls are all right but they are girls and there is no more to be said about that.'

There is no doubt that it was a different man that came back from the War. This was not such an uncommon occurrence in those years. The mass of the population had not suffered any of the horrors of war and this applied particularly to the women. Consequently the psychological effects on many men were not observed or allowed for, with very unhappy results. In the letter my father wrote and never finished in 1921, as a sort of aftermath to the Gallipoli letter, he says, 'And only yesterday I was writing to you in a tragic vein, it appears. Well, the father that so wrote to you died, as he expected to die. The one that writes to you now is no more than the husk, living out a life that he finds infinitely wearisome . . .' He was only 41.

This feeling, strongest soon after the War, remained with him in the following years, despite his laughter and fun and interests. Maybe it was only the poet's loss of youthful inspiration and the final loss of youth itself. Maybe such giving-in to introspective gloom was a defence against laziness, which he himself admitted was the family's besetting sin. However, he still had a great many enthusiasms ahead, not least Africa, and in particular Kenya. After the War he and my mother went on a safari that was the start of a quiet and consuming love affair with that country. From 1923 onwards it was his custom to travel after the Christmas holidays until the salmon fishing started on the Dee on April 1st (it was later altered to March). He made several journeys to the Belgian Congo and explored the Etruri Forest, as well as buying the land in Kenya and acquiring the businesses that later resulted in his having a controlling interest in the East African newspapers. This led to his meeting and friendship with Ewart Grogan, that remarkable man who in the 1890s had walked from the Cape to Cairo.

He felt that it was his duty to help this colonial country and this strong feeling never wavered. He loved the place and the people and was always thinking of new ideas to bring the nation along towards a more civilised life. He was naturally opposed to creating temptations on which the Africans would spend their money and so be obliged to keep on working.

This period of his life also included his children's pantomimes, which show quite another side of his character. These he enjoyed hugely, as did all the cast and, one likes to think, some of the audience. They are very witty and he seemed to be able to turn his hand to writing a thriller as easily as a blank verse *Sleeping Beauty* à la Shakespeare. He wrote mostly at night and later was able to reel off the speeches without having to look up the original. The pantomimes were played on a stage built at the far end of the Long Gallery at Chirk. This was highly convenient because at the side was a bedroom called the King's Room that became a sort of Green Room where we all changed. Usually my mother produced the plays and both my parents painted the scenery, sometimes helped by my father's friend from Eton days, Harry Morritt. The advantage my father had was that he knew what cast he was writing for and what their capabilities were according to their age. In 1929 we did *Puss and Brutes* à la Edgar Wallace. It was in this pantomime that my schoolfriend, Brian Johnston, and his brother Chris took part. Brian is of course the Test-match commentator on radio.

The normal cast consisted of us children and the Ridley family who always came to stay for Christmas. Bubbles, the eldest, was sadly killed in the war. Then came Katherine, Constantine and Oliver, also now dead. My mother said in her book that I was a natural actor and I must admit to having always enjoyed it, as did Bubbles. All the others were not so keen though they played their part and I'm sure enjoyed the general fun. Our greatest problem as children was to get an audience. By the time we had done one performance for local friends and neighbours and one for the household and tenantry, we were hard up for anyone else. On one occasion Phyllis Neilson Terry (a proper actress) was induced to produce the pantomime. This resulted in a lot of tears and tantrums – perhaps her professionalism was a bit too much for us, and I hardly think that she can have enjoyed it much either.

My father's year followed an orderly design, as after the Christmas pantomime he would travel until March, then fish during the school holidays till May. He reverted to his love of yachts and although the ones he had in the post-war years were much smaller and less elaborate, still they were able to take most of the family on various cruises. The *Ethelreda* took all the family from Oban round Ardnamurchan (memories of horror to most of us) and, an unforgettable experience, right through the Caledonian Canal. Summers were always glorious then. The autumns were occupied with shooting parties and hawking, both at Chirk and Newmarket. During this period occurred the strange case that led to my father resigning from the Jockey Club – I believe the only person ever to have done so. The subject was never mentioned by him in my hearing.

Apparently my father disapproved of the proposed election of a certain gentleman who became possibly the most influential man on the British Turf in later years. He disapproved because of certain things this gentleman was supposed to have been involved in many years earlier. My father was adamant and when various senior members said to him, 'Do you realise he is Master of the – (a famous pack of fox-hounds)?' my father replied, 'I suppose that if Beelzebub rode well to hounds you would elect him!' Many years later, when I started racing after my father's death, the same gentleman proposed me for the Jockey Club as if to say, 'Let bygones be bygones'. He was always very nice to me, so I think it better to leave this little social drama to be lost in the mists of time.

As their children grew up my mother and father seemed to go their separate ways – I do not mean in the accepted and vulgar sense that their marriage was 'on the rocks'. It was that their interests and friends were totally different, and neither seemed willing or able to conform to the other's tastes. My father's loneliness increased, his mind became more and more absorbed by the follies of the day and how to try and lead a few chosen people back on the right path, so that they in their turn could spread the right ideas throughout their particular lives. This developed into his part in the English Mistery movement. I think his feelings could be summed up by the idea that when human life is on a wrong basis, the most that legislation can effect is a more equitable distribution of the resulting evils.

There is little doubt that the Mistery attracted some very able young men and influenced a great many more. It suffered in some ways by having some odd characters at the top. William Sanderson, the author of *Statecraft* – 'a treatise on the concerns of our sovereign Lord the King', was the first chancellor and the movement's philosopher, but was not good enough to collate and put down the basic tenets of faith. He was succeeded by Anthony Ludovici who became besotted by the concept of 'Aristocracy' and whose best-known work was *A Defence of Aristocracy*.

The best way to give an idea of what this movement was is to quote a speech of my father's given in 1933, headed, 'The Value of the English Mistery'.

The only thing in England that can have constant value in peace and war is the teaching of the English Mistery. It is from this alone that we can get any idea of direction. In the havoc of party government the need of direction is demonstrated by pains endured for lack of it. Nothing good can happen to a man or a nation except when going in the right direction. It is only too obvious that there is no longer an institution to point the way. No doubt we shall again

respond to the stimulus of war and defeat the King's enem-
ies, but without the English Mistery we shall certainly again
betray the King's peace.

The Mistery teaches us how to find the right direction,
and how to build a social structure for our permanent wel-
fare. We have tried to choose our path by having elections,
with the result that every decision is reversed by the next.
Opinions multiply and all are bewildered. We have tried to
find a moral basis in theory, and have but succeeded in the
destruction of manners. The end of it is that we never
ascribe our policies and legislation in war or peace to any
genuine or consistent motive. Our actions, whether good or
bad, fail in consequence for lack of faith.

The only permanent basis for a political society is reli-
gion, which is the binding-together for a certain purpose,
and the binding back to ancestral wisdom, so that the reve-
lation of tradition may teach us what that purpose ought to
be. Nothing in itself is either good or evil, except in relation
to that purpose, and we can leave abstract morality to the
Romans. Our business is to find out the worth of everything
for our purpose. Anything may be good or bad, or good and
bad, according as it is used, and knowledge has no value
except for a purpose. Science is useless or dangerous, except
when it is subject to valuation, and controlled by worship.
Any other doctrine results either in anarchy or in the theory
that might is right. Might is in fact right, if it is in fact right
or straight, and not crooked.

If those who do not fight in the war fail to keep this
teaching alive they will betray all who are fighting and leave
them no more hope on their return than the survivors of the
last war. In these anxious days reflect again on the tests by
which you can know that the English Mistery is genuine.

How are we to know that this is really a genuine movement and not one of those fleeting things which spring up in
the night and vanish within about a fortnight, to be heard of

no more? I will take a test which one of our greatest mora-
lists and philosophers has suggested as the distinction which
is to be made between the things which are real and the
things which are sham. He said that there were three points
by which you can know that. The first is whether they tend
to order, because order is the first essential of reality. That
the Mistery does and always will do; but admittedly that
could be said of a great many intellectual systems which
have been invented, and which bother us to-day. The next
test is that of completeness. If a person produces to you an
absolutely complete, cut-and-dried theory, in every particular an absolutely finished article, then it is a sham, because
there is no movement of any value which must be other than
a living organism, and which has not to apply itself to
different situations as they arise. Again that applies to the
Mistery. It is not a cut, dried and worked-out hard-and-fast
theory into which all humanity has to be thrust. It is merely
the application of certain principles which we believe to be
inherent in our Royalist instincts and traditions, to such
situations as may arise. The third and final test of this philosopher is the test of reserve. The philosopher and moralist in
question said that the final and absolute test of reality is:
Does it come out into the open and bang the big drum? If it
does, it is a fraud. That ultimate test I think applies to the
Mistery more than any other. We have not trumpeted in the
market-place and we do not propose ever to trumpet in the
market-place. By that reserve, I think, men will know us for
the perfectly genuine thing that we are.

My father enjoyed meeting and talking to intelligent young
men of the day and the movement brought him back to the
intellectual concerns of his earlier years. He made a valiant
attempt to stop at least some good brains rushing down the
Gadarene slope to disaster amongst the party politicians.
It was about the end of the 1920s that he began to take more

than a passing interest in painting. He had always sketched on all his trips and had a small but pleasant talent. Now he decided he would start at the beginning and learn the craft properly. He acquired a mews studio not five minutes' walk from Seaford House and hired himself a teacher. He spent many hours – very happy ones – drawing, and gradually improved his technique until one day he was persuaded to have a one-man show in London, where the majority of his pictures sold for charity. I well remember the shock of walking in one day and seeing him painting a model in the nude who was a genuine piebald. There may be a word for this extraordinary figuration when seen on a human, but I don't know it and I have never seen another case like it.

During this painting period he became very interested in things psychic, and attended many seances and automatic hand-writing sessions. He was greatly interested in such matters but was wise and steady enough not to be carried away by emotions. I believe that in the final analysis he was sure that most things that were inexplicable had a unity of explanation on a plane that is at present outside our understanding, and also that it is extremely dangerous to play with these things without some knowledge of what may lie behind. He was still a voracious reader and was influenced by the thoughts both of Oswald Spengler's *Decline of the West* and also of Ouspensky's *New Model of the Universe*, and the theories of Dunne in *Experiment with Time*. As the years rolled by he became more of a recluse and spent the majority of his time alone, painting, reading and writing.

It was during the 1930s that he started to get interested in shipping. This was not in any way a business concern, except academically; rather a feeling that it was a worthwhile area, as war was looming whilst the British Merchant Navy was in serious straits. It was also sentimental, as he loved ships and the whole atmosphere of the docks. Like so many of his ventures in life, this was something started at exactly the right time and would no doubt have been a huge financial success if management had measured up to the standards of conduct set by the Chairman. Unfortunately, although many innovations that were of great benefit to the Merchant Navy were made – particularly the first ships with all single cabins amidship for members of the crew and stewards – the climate after the war was not correctly appreciated. The shipping booms during the Korean and Suez wars were thought usual, but eventually the strain of inflation proved too much for the business to carry on alone. My father fortunately did not live to see this dream wrecked.

During the Second World War his life was a sad and lonely one, confined to the Home Guard in North Wales. Curiously, towards the end of the war, it so happened that old Poss Myddelton, from whom my father had taken the lease of Chirk, came to stay. They were together there when my parents were obliged to leave and move up to Dean Castle in Ayrshire. In the last months of the war I ran into Ryd Myddelton, Poss's son, and he asked, 'What would you do if you were me?' To which I replied, 'You will do the same to your son as my father has to me: bring him up at Chirk, so that it is his home, and then you will not be able to continue and history will be repeated.' Sadly, so it came to pass and Chirk was handed over to the National Trust some years later, although Ryd's widow, Lady Margaret Myddelton, still lives in part of the castle and has done a wonderful job improving the garden. Fortunately she is allowed by the Trust to advise and carry out her ideas. The castle is well looked after, and I still go into the rooms in my mind and run down the familiar corridors.

CHAPTER THREE

My Mother

M Y MOTHER'S FATHER WAS THE SON OF AN immigrant Jewish Dutchman called Marcus Van Raalte who managed to make a fortune in the City. My grandfather, Charles, was more interested in painting and music and one day met a student called Florence Clow when visiting the Royal Academy. In 1886 they were married and at first lived in London with his parents. Then after a spell at Aldenham Abbey near Watford, where Charles could both hunt and get up to the City easily, in 1901 they bought Brownsea Island in Poole Harbour, in Dorset. Charles was quite a collector of furniture, books and tapestries, and especially of early musical instruments, which today can be seen at Dean Castle. He was a JP and Mayor of Poole. He stood for Parliament as a Conservative for East Dorset and was secretly relieved when he failed to get in by twenty votes. He died in Calcutta in 1908 and is buried at Brownsea.

His wife, my grandmother, whom I can remember well, was a good-looking and talented lady. She painted attractive water colours and some miniatures. Her failings, however, were that she was an unmitigated snob and rather stupid. She had three children: two daughters, of whom the eldest was my mother, and one son. My mother was very musical and very determined, and at an early age, took up the violin. However, it was eventually singing that became her great love; also singing was considered more suitable by my grandmother. Florence thought everything had to be 'comme il faut' and she was determined her son Nony should join a Guards regiment. He was totally unsuited to this as he was a brilliant engineer and motor racing driver. This battle Florence fortunately lost.

My mother made a great success of singing. She had perfect pitch and a very pleasant voice and worked hard, first with Olga Lynn and later for a short period with Jean de Reszke. She performed at many festivals as well as at the Royal Albert Hall and other major halls. I think she was very hurt when a number of professionals said she was taking the bread out of their mouths and I am sure this hastened her retirement.

During her upbringing at Brownsea she was very influenced by the Infante D'Orleans Bourbon, or Prince Ali as we knew him. Prince Ali was always determined to show that royalty could succeed and be competent in the outside world. He was also a fitness fanatic and this appealed to my mother who delighted in feats of endurance. In those days she sailed a lot and thought nothing of swimming over to the Haven Hotel on the mainland, a distance of at least a mile. Brownsea Island is remembered nowadays as the place where the Boy Scout movement was founded by Baden-Powell. My mother and her sister Poots were quite young when this took place, but I believe they raided the camp in a mild way and were duly arrested and reprimanded by the great man. I have a small book got up by my grandmother that includes photographs of those present at the camp and the telegrams and letters sent between Baden-Powell and my grandmother.

My mother was a very capable lady indeed and became an inspired organiser. For her, the moment to prove herself came when war broke out in 1914. She had already had twins, Bronwen and myself, and Elizabeth was born in December 1914. (Three more daughters followed later.) Mama was determined to get into the action and she overcame any obstacles to set up a hospital with Mary Herbert in Egypt. This turned out to be a huge success and it has always been a surprise to me that she was so anti-catholic, since Mary Herbert was a Roman Catholic, as were all her family. Mary was the wife of Aubrey Herbert and their daughter Laura married Evelyn Waugh.

After the war Mama took to hunting and enjoyed many days in Leicestershire as well as at Chirk with the Wynstay pack. She travelled to Kenya with my father and had a really wonderful safari. I have no idea why she didn't return there as she never tired of talking about all the stalking and the habits of the animals. She says in her own book that the reason was that she associated Kenya with open air and walking and that safaris were now motor rides. My father had built a house and home there and it was no longer the same. I personally take leave to doubt that was the real reason, but I might well be wrong.

It was in the early 1920s that my parents drifted apart, although they remained on good terms and our lives were not affected in any way. One of the troubles was that my father had always derived great pleasure from his discussions with such people as Bernard Shaw, George Moore, G. K. Chesterton, Augustus John and the like. My mother was not really able to keep up with this heady stuff and gradually, even perhaps unconsciously, drove them away so that the people who came to stay tended to be more and more her friends.

I have often thought of my mother as going through phases, as is expected of the young: 'Oh, its just a phase she is going through.' One of the most obvious was what all of us children would have called her 'Louise' phase. Louise Edvina was born a French Canadian and had achieved considerable success as an opera singer. No doubt singing is what brought them together, but it became an all-consuming relationship. Louise had a shop in Cannes where she sold lamps and small items of furniture. My mother and she used to go off together to Italy to buy things for it. These were suited to the South of France, but terribly out of keeping at Chirk, where they were apt to creep into bedrooms. Many people, including my own family, would not agree with me, but I think Mama had bad taste and no real feeling for decor. Louise used to make us laugh when she sang at the piano such modern songs as, 'If you like a Ukelele lady, Ukelele lady like a you'. She sang them in the grand manner and they sounded absurd, like asking Callas to sing 'You're the Cream in my Coffee'. She was kind at heart, but had a very strong influence over my mother, even pertaining to her children. Louise was asked to speak to me about getting married and I was greeted with no applause when I answered, 'What do you know about it? You've been married five times.'

Another phase was referred to as the 'Moke' phase. 'Moke' was Mrs Fitzclarence, a very different cup of tea to Louise. She seemed to be permanently around and, whereas Louise used to dominate Mama, that is to say Mama did what Louise wanted, in Moke's case it was the reverse. She fagged for Mama and seemed to be always at her beck and call. In later years, my mother used to go on cruises or visit countries in South America, where she picked up an amazing amount of perfectly dreadful people who used to come and stay, though totally out of place.

Mama was still very active and used to terrify me by doing cartwheels on the roof at Chirk, at which she excelled. She also took up flying, together with my sister Priscilla, and got her licence. She was convinced that landing a plane must be like bringing a boat alongside, and I daresay she was right as she learnt that aspect quite safely: navigation was another matter. On one occasion she flew off in her little Puss Moth to Scotland and was expected back at Chirk on a certain day. No Mama, and we all waited rather anxiously, until eventually the telephone rang: 'Darling, I'm in Northern Ireland, I never saw the sea!'

I'm afraid that a lot of what I have said sounds rather disparaging, but Mama had a very strong character and dominated her daughters, who more or less did what they were told. My mother told them not to be nice to Nucci when she came to

47

stay with her father prior to our official engagement, and this has always been hurtful to me. Mama's Jewish blood made her rather anti-primogeniture and she always felt my sisters were badly done-by compared to myself, which financially was strictly true, but the same applied to all English landed families. However, she had a large amount of good points and was a real expert at entertaining and giving parties. I used to go round with her and learn how to place the chairs and all that sort of thing. She was a perfectionist and everything had to be 'just so'. The result was always outstanding. She undoubtedly helped a lot of musical aspirants on their way and raised money for many worthy causes, especially Queen Charlotte's Maternity Hospital. My mother includes in her book the story which inspired the Queen Charlotte's Ball. It describes how Queen Charlotte, wife of George III and mother of George IV and William IV, had a Birthday Ball each year at St James's Palace. She liked to have a birthday cake with candles lit to the music of the March from Handel's *Judas Maccabeus*. She would then cut the cake. The Queen took a personal and practical interest in poor women, whether ill, in childbirth or homeless. So Queen Charlotte's Hospital, the first woman's hospital, was named after her. It was thought fitting at this Ball to pay tribute to the gracious Queen and to re-enact her birthday party. A guest of honour represents Queen Charlotte, to whom the maids of honour make their obeisance, to the playing of the music the Queen herself chose.

It is a pity that my mother's name has become so firmly associated with that dance. People deride it now who were only too pleased to attend it in the past. It was really a very clever idea to start with, as no invitations had to be sent out. Mothers used to write and ask for their daughters to attend, so that one secretary could deal with that side of things. There were virtually no overheads as businesses like Jacksons of Piccadilly used to give their services for free – the advent of sponsorship. As I had five younger sisters and four daughters, I have probably attended more of the Balls than anyone, and my mother often asked me to act as host in later years.

Her strong will and character were best exemplified in her last days. She had a slight heart problem – she was 85 and I went to see her in her flat in Eaton Square a day or two after Christmas. She was sitting up in her drawing room and full of chat. I asked her where she would like to go in the New Year; she usually spent a week or two in France or Italy. She answered, 'Darling, I am not sure whether I want to live or die. On New Year's Eve I shall make up my mind.' I naturally said, 'Rubbish', and changed the subject. On New Year's Eve her doctor rang and said, 'Your mother is dying but I don't quite know why.' 'I do', I replied. 'She has made up her mind.'

CHAPTER FOUR

Childhood at Chirk

NO MAN CAN BE TOO CAREFUL IN CHOSING HIS parents; I doubt whether I would have chosen mine as a combination had I had such a choice. My father and mother were both people of exceptional merit and character, but so divergent were their attributes that they were most likely to produce offspring that fell somewhere in the middle and had neither of their extreme abilities and characteristics. My father was a shy man with a powerful intellect and great all-round ability; in many ways very near to the rounded man who could do most things pretty well. He was incapable of showing emotion, which does not mean that he felt none, but he was not outwardly warm, in fact he was very self-contained. My mother was half-Jewish and had some of the flair of that race. She had a very quick grasp of essentials but no capacity for studying a subject in depth. She also showed no emotion and I honestly do not believe she knew the meaning of warmth in personal relationships. She was very efficient, strong-willed and enthusiastic. She placed people very quickly into mental pigeon holes from which they rarely escaped. The fusion of these two beings produced children who were sometimes very emotional but could not show it, or who were quite cold and hadn't got it to show. I leave my family to decide in which category they are, or were!

I have neither my father's intellect nor my mother's will-power, only his shyness and some of her slickness. I was very emotional and uncontrolled, but suffered from a total lack of warmth from my parents; they showed kindness in abundance, and everything except understanding. There is nothing unusual in this, except for the individual himself. The lack of warmth had a far greater effect on my life than being brought up in the 'West Wing' and presented to bore the grown-ups at five o'clock in a satin tunic. There was no doubt that my being the eldest and only son presented my parents with a greater problem than it did myself. They went out of their way to find what they considered the toughest preparatory school, so that I should not be spoilt. I do not believe that by nature I have ever been spoilt, so perhaps they were successful. My mother was full of notions about what I would do, or become. One of her obsessions was that I was bound to marry a chorus girl and therefore all steps should be taken to see that this did not occur. Her methods were a little eccentric. When I was about 14, for a year or so she took me to rehearsals of musical comedies in London. The idea was that I would see little Mavis, Gladys and Deirdre in their knickers and note that some had dirty necks and take against their sisters in the future. But I was quite oblivious to any faults or charms they had and amused myself learning tricks in the wings from such comics as Lupino Lane. On the first night I would mildly embarrass my parents by waving at the girls in their sparkling get-up. I did not marry one, so who knows whether the system is useful or not?

Chirk Castle was a five-towered 13th-Century border castle with a large rectangular courtyard and, as a home, was everything glorious. I believe that I could still run round it in the dark, although I have only been there once, quite recently, in the last thirty years. Actually this exaggerates slightly as a wall now obstructs a passage where the National Trust caretaker's flat starts.

I should like to pass over my extreme youth as quickly as possible as it is ultimately only interesting to the person himself and in no way to others. By the time I and my sister Bronwen were four years old, there were already two more girls, so we were up-graded to the school-room and handed over to a French governess and a French maid. There were a few false starts until we were finally settled in with Mademoiselle Klein and Mariette. Despite Mademoiselle's cries of 'petit crapaud' and extreme discipline, there is no doubt that she was a very good teacher. Bronwen and I used to be incensed because we were convinced that she stole food and sent it in mysterious brown paper parcels to a certain Mrs Bun of 14 Unthank Road, Norwich, an address written on my heart. The castle itself was presided over by a butler called Harper who had started as a bookmaker's clerk, a rather surprising change of jobs. He had apparently taken a bet on the telephone after the permitted time, which had won at 40–1, and spent a great many years paying it off. His predecessor, Cover, had a slightly larger tummy and a golden chain. Harper once bought a pedometer and assured my mother that he walked an average of eight miles a day without leaving the castle. This is quite likely to be accurate as it was strictly forbidden for any servant to use the courtyard and so they had to walk all the way round, through drawing rooms, long galleries, chapels, etc.

I was educated by Mademoiselle Klein from the age of 4 till 9, before I went to Summerfields. During those years our parents were quite often away for long periods and this left us to the in-fighting between the nursery (housing Elizabeth, Priscilla and Migse – later called Gaenor), the school-room (containing Bronwen and me and later Elizabeth), the steward's room (housing the butler and housekeeper), and anyone else who cared to have a finger in the pie. Due to a merciful God, the majority of my memories are pleasant and the bad days seem to have vanished slowly as the years passed. The overriding impact of the time on me was made by the castle, the wonderful oak trees and the space.

The general routine of the day started with lessons in the school-room (the room now used by Margaret Myddelton as her dining room). I seem to remember poor Elizabeth spent a lot of time under the table, presumably to escape Mademoiselle's 'gifles' – slaps. Between the two big windows was a bureau-bookcase and on the third shelf Mademoiselle kept a blue box in which were stored our fines. I can't remember what we were fined for or what we paid with, but Bronwen and I always had a strong desire to get at that box. Later in the morning we used to go riding, which was much more agreeable. There were two ponies in particular, called Taffy and Roney, and the groom was Mr Roberts. In those days the seasons seemed to behave in the way they are meant to – that is the sun shone in the summer and in the winter there was snow, and we could be pulled about on sledges by the ponies.

We had a little house down by the lake where we were allowed to cook. I considered myself an expert in the production of hot chocolate. Why this feat was considered special I have no recollection, but it seems to have been completely accepted by my sisters. Like most children we kept rabbits and we had a very big wired-in compound for them in the wood. One day my father returned with a large number of amazingly marked rabbits, some green and some striped like tigers. It transpired that he had got them from an experimental breeding place, I think at Cambridge. They lived merrily for a time until the dogs managed to force their way in and, although they killed a few, a fair number escaped to the woods. Later in the year the local master of hounds, of a very peppery disposition, was a guest at a shoot. After a couple of glasses of port he sallied forth to the first drive after lunch. Lo and behold a green rabbit and his striped companion appeared, whereupon the master hurled his gun to the ground shouting, 'I've got them again', and then disappeared at a fast but unsteady trot.

I believe that I asked to go to school; if this is correct it was not the last time that I made a moderate choice, but I suppose having five sisters and a governess was a bit stifling. I hated my preparatory school; it was very strict and I only really survived because I was quite good at most games. I made two great friends there, neither of whom I ever saw again. The period was shortly after the First War and probably many of the masters were somewhat akin to those described by Evelyn Waugh. One exception was L. A. G. Strong, later to become a successful novelist and man of letters. He had great charm and I am sure all my contemporaries remember both his acting and his history pictures. The latter were founded on bad puns but were extremely useful in remembering names of battles, etc. Another memorable feature were the dreadful outside lavatories, mysteriously called The Vinery. Under the rows of seats flowed a small rivulet that presumably ended up in the Cherwell. I had one advantage at Summerfields and that was that I could speak French, as Bronwen and I used to play in it as children. Mademoiselle Klein and Mariette both came from Alsace-Lorraine and had an infuriating habit of conversing in the local patois, which of course defeated us. However, at school, despite the fact that my grammar was weak I could produce the answer even if I didn't know it was a good example of 'ne' before the subjunctive. In the two bottom forms at Summerfields we were taught by two sisters called Miss Hill Major and Miss Hill Minor; they were very understanding and I am sure set many a frightened boy on the right path. Many years later, around 1942, I ran into these two dear old ladies in Yorkshire. They were very excited and said to me, 'Isn't little Archie doing well!' It took me a short while to recognise Field Marshal Sir Archibald Wavell.

The Great War started two years after I was born and in my father's absence, it was left to my mother to put me down for Eton. Mathematics, at which she rather fancied herself, were not really her forte and she entered me for a year too early. Most boys at Summerfields who were not morons, were supposed to attempt a scholarship; good ones were obtained to Eton, Winchester and other leading schools with the utmost regularity. For each one the school had a half-holiday. As far as I was concerned, I was undoubtedly well educated at Summerfields, as I really disliked getting the cane on my hand for a bad construing in Latin. (One was obliged to be very careful to get one's thumbs out of the way. It is amusing to think what would happen today if these methods were put into practice in our modern schools. I have a strong belief that it would be both salutary and effective.) But thanks to the mix-up over dates I had to take the common entrance to Eton in September, a year early, and passed high without much difficulty, a great vindication of Dr Williams and not due to any special ability on my part. Dr Cyril Williams was to all intents and purposes the real Headmaster at Summerfields and taught the Classics. He was rather red-faced and very strict, but obviously got results. He took over the headmastership from Allington, known as the Bear, in 1927 when the Bear blacked out in chapel and had to be led away.

Two incidents that had some effect on later years took place during these Summerfields days. Amongst my father's friends in the theatre was Phyllis Neilson Terry, whose parents, Fred Terry and Julia Nelson, were still touring in the *Scarlet Pimpernel* at the time. Phyllis was playing in Oxford and was the first person to take me out of school. I can still remember the mild furore that this caused. The wife of the headmaster, Mrs Allington, was very deaf and used one of those old-fashioned trumpets. Having to describe who, and what, Phyllis was, aged nine, was daunting. Her arrival was nice and theatrical as she was tall and splendid looking. I rather think my stock rose after that episode. It was perhaps also the first inkling I had of my attraction to the stage. This attraction has been studiously sublimated over the years, but I can have my dreams of what might have been.

The second event, that started a taste that *has* been allowed to fructify, was a result of the school going down with measles. My parents were in Africa and my guardian, with commendable promptitude, removed me to stay with an aunt of my father's at The Old Rectory at Snailwell, near Newmarket.

Needless to say I immediately contracted the disease but was somewhere much nicer than the dreaded sanatorium. I then developed a poisoned finger and the whole stay lasted much longer than expected. Aunt Cissy was one of the most delightful ladies I have ever known, but was always rather overshadowed by her husband, the rector, Funny Uncle to us, who must have been one of the last of the so-called Sporting Parsons. He looked after my father's stud at Snailwell and came regularly to Chirk to fish in March and April. I was given the severest ticking off by him for playing bezique with my Irish nurse on Sunday while the household was at church. However, when convalescing, I used to go to the Heath to see the horses and hear the likely winners from the jockeys. I was hooked and have remained so ever since.

CHAPTER FIVE

Eton and Some Islands

MY ARRIVAL AT ETON IN JANUARY 1925 started the way it was to continue, that is to say badly. I was, for some reason unknown, very uppity, and soon decided that it was ridiculous that a mysterious headmaster should preside over us new boys without us ever speaking to him or ever seeing him, except rarely in the distance. The headmaster was the celebrated Dr Cyril Alington. I chose to write and post him a letter to this effect and suggested that he might like to come to tea with me and my new friends in our House. Why I ever sent the letter I don't know; probably egged on, together with the usual bravado. Cyril Alington's reply and the action he took were a very good example of his methods and his humour, which I was able to appreciate as time went on, though usually from the wrong side of the birch. He wrote a charming letter explaining that the school had over eleven hundred boys and that anyway he was entertaining two bishops at the weekend, and would I like to come to breakfast on Sunday? This brooked no refusal. I doubt whether I have ever been so frightened since. He was indeed entertaining bishops, and several others as well. His daughter, Elizabeth (Lady Home), was there and I believe had a little sympathy for me. No one else did, nor was meant to. I had to sit on the Headmaster's right and read aloud a description of a football match, full of dreadful old journalese. I seem to remember spluttering out 'and from an inside pass Jack netted the leathern sphere'. I suppose the press at the time was still fighting its way out of Augustus Sala's, 'downing a dozen

57

succulent bivalves'. I was duly made to look very foolish and if I looked it, I felt it a hundredfold more. Very salutary and I only wish I had learnt faster.

I should like to pass over the next three years, which to date have been the most unsatisfactory ones of my life. I had advantages in that I wasn't stupid and was quite good at most games, yet I squandered all this because of an ingrained laziness or lack of will. The long and short of the matter is that I was a mess at Eton, certainly up to the age of sixteen; I cheated and felt no remorse and when threatened with the sack – 'you have come to the end of your tether', is what Dr Alington once greeted me with – I always managed to put on a tearful act and wriggle out. Here is a letter from my father to my mother dated 29th July, 1926.

Dear Margot,

I enclose John's reports. As you will see they are uniformly deplorable from beginning to end. This on top of his failing to write is a little too much. I'm afraid he seems to have all his father's failings and none of his very few virtues.

Of course we may have overrated him and he is really only a rather stupid and untidy boy but it may be he is upset by the beginning of the age of puberty. But I must say the lack of ambition and generally wooliness of character is profoundly disappointing.

Try and shake the little brute up.

Yours

T.

It would be nice to put it all down to the age of puberty, if it wasn't for the fact that this is a universal stage and affects everyone. My parents, and particularly my father, were rightly disgusted and decided, in an attempt to make me mend my ways, that I should have a tutor in the holidays. In fact, I had two. The first of these unfortunates was called Mr Lillingston, who later became a well-known and highly successful house-master at Harrow. He arrived at Chirk when my father was only due back the next evening. In the morning I sallied forth with the headkeeper, George Wright, and my tutor to shoot rabbits using ferrets. I doubt whether this rather tricky pursuit had entered the life of Mr Lillingston and he distinguished himself by not only shooting a ferret but peppering the keeper as well, who reported very unfavourably to my father. I think he was lucky to avoid having to take the midnight train from Chester, which was the threatened fate of guests who over-stepped the mark. I don't remember the threat ever being carried out but it was part of the world we lived in. My second tutor was 'Rasher' Bacon, as he came to be called. He was one of the first pupils at the new Police College at Hendon and he rose to hold the highest position in the Police Force.

There were marvellous holidays in those days. When I was quite small we were sent for a short stay to Aberdovey. Bron-wen and I decided that we would swap clothes and see if we could fool anyone. We succeeded rather well. The strange part of this episode is that we were not remotely alike, either physi-cally or in temperament. Bronwen was a lot taller than me until we were about fifteen, and she excelled at riding and reading. She devoured every book in sight and very early on had demolished Thomas Hardy and the rest of the modern classics, whereas those treasures did not appeal to me until much later. Bronwen and Elizabeth were both excellent in the saddle and won innumerable prizes, even at Olympia, which was the top in those days. I, on the other hand, was rather frightened and never totally gave myself up to it. One incident had a lot to do with this. I was run away with, on what seemed a huge grey horse, and nearly disappeared down a precipice. Nobody seemed either to notice or to care.

Sometimes we went to stay with my mother's mother, Florence Van Raalte, living as a widow on Brownsea Island. It was about eight miles round and had two fresh-water lakes, a small golf course, a church, fine woods, a small but lovely beach and a large Victorian castle. She used to invite all the foreign royalties who where in the country to stay; and they came, I can only suppose because an island afforded privacy and because it was also fun, with its bathing and fishing. She was known, rather obviously, as Mrs Van Royalty. Her sort of snobbery hurts nobody and I expect she got a lot of pleasure counting queens and kings and princesses. On one occasion, Bronwen and I arrived alone and went down to lunch (alone probably meant with one governess and a maid). We were, with my grandmother, three ordinary folk with twenty-eight royals. I can hear the shade of Chips Channon grinding his teeth. At first we did not know who was who so my mother devised the idea of saying 'wasps' if a royal was approaching, and then we knew to bow or to curtsey.

One afternoon at Brownsea, Elizabeth climbed onto a glass roof on the pier and fell through. She was extremely badly cut and had to be operated on. My mother was obliged to give the anaesthetic herself. After several weeks, we returned to Chirk and the first day Elizabeth was allowed to play with us she fell off the swing. I shall always believe that my rather drastic ministrations finally broke her collarbone. This was not noticed until we went to meet my mother off the train in the evening.

The other place by the sea we went for holidays was to the island of Shona in Loch Moidart on the West Coast of Scotland. This island my father had given to my mother and she was mad about it, with good reason. It was again about eight miles in circumference, but rose to a high peak in the centre. The house was not beautiful, but cosy and roomy, and we went for picnics to marvellous sandy beaches. Once we went in a launch with friends miles from anywhere and to our horror a butler appeared with a table and chairs. We were more accustomed to eating chocolate while paddling. The journey to Shona was a great part of the excitement. The train left about

10.00 pm from London; a marvellous breakfast consisting of porridge, fried eggs and bacon was put into our carriages in small hampers at Crianlarich, and we reached Fort William at 10.00 am. Here one changed and went for a short journey to Glenfinnan. I believe that Glenfinnan is the wettest place in the British Isles and if any witnesses are required to prove the point, my sisters and I would step forward in unison. Here, for some reason, one waited about two hours in a dismal little boarding house and had lunch, before boarding the good ship *Clanranald* and sailing for two hours down Loch Shiel till one reached Acharacle. Then again a drive of about forty minutes, when the island was sighted and horns were blown to attract the launch to come and fetch us. On other occasions we used to arrive by yacht; although this was a great pleasure, the fear of going round Ardnamurchan laid a large lump in one's tummy, as we were usually all sick. During lunches at Shona my father used, sometimes, to start telling us a story and these stories became serials which continued day after day, usually about the exploits of Cuchullin, after whom the mountains in Skye are named.

When I was still at Summerfields, I contracted some illness which, in my mother's opinion, necessitated a change of air and she took me to Cannes in the South of France. I suppose I must have been about eleven or twelve. The reason for Cannes was Louise Edvina's antique shop there. I must, on this occasion, have been a burden to my mother, but she got rid of me one morning by handing me over to go shopping with Sir Hugo de Bathe (Suggie as he was known) whose claim to fame was being the husband of Lily Langtry. I can still remember with a certain amount of embarrassment, the choosing of suits for the elegant elderly gentleman and the exotic satin linings that had to go in them.

One evening I was taken to dine with some old lady in the hills behind Cannes. There was a large number of people and I was pleased when dinner was over. Then a lady and her husband came up to me and said, 'How would you like to come home with us tonight and stay a few days?' – panic stations! When my mother appeared, to my unutterable horror, she said that she thought it an excellent idea and off I went into the night with total strangers in a strange land. They were in fact Mr and Mrs Lloyd Osbourne and he had been a collaborator with Robert Louis Stevenson in writing *The Wrong Box*. They were extremely nice and I swam and was spoilt and not too despondent when my mother did not show up for three days.

When I was a little older, another occasion arose when it was deemed the right thing for me to go abroad for my health. This time my mother excelled herself by sending me to meet a Russian who played the violin in a cinema in Cannes. He had been a tutor to a nephew, or lover of an aunt, probably both, and together we were to visit Corsica. This extraordinary trip started by hiring a car in Ajaccio to drive across the island to Bastia in the north-east. I was astonished to find Sacha practising with a revolver in the hills. He said there were bandits about and I am sure he was right, then as now. All went well until Sacha, coming too fast round a corner, struck a herd of goats. We had to put the car on the train, a small-gauge affair, all the way to Bastia. After a few days there we took the train back with the car still on board and broken beyond repair. Whilst in the station, we saw in a siding a coach of great antiquity: very ornate, with sofas and ormolu lamps. We asked what it would cost to attach it to our train and, to our surprise, the price was very small. This was irresistible and we travelled in great style, drawing large crowds at each small station where we stopped.

When we returned to Marseilles it was our intention to go to Spain, but unfortunately Sacha only had a Nansen pass, rather than a proper passport, and that was not acceptable. So we decided at lunch to go to Switzerland, and departed for Geneva with no fixed plans. However, once there, another of

Sacha's more extreme performances hurried our departure. In a bar opposite the League of Nations, he got rather tight and, drawing out that dreaded revolver, proceeded to shoot all the bottles behind the barman. We both ran out and somehow escaped to our hotel. A little later we went to the station and bought tickets to the Kleine Scheidegg before the police caught up with us. No doubt it was good experience, but I question whether my mother would have approved had she known.

CHAPTER SIX

Kenya

I LEFT ETON AT CHRISTMAS 1930. IT WOULD HAVE been the normal thing to stay on until the end of the summer term in 1931 and go on to University in October. However, there did not seem to be any point as I had passed the exams that were necessary and I was not a candidate for the cricket eleven. Nowadays a gap of at least nine months between school and university is the normal and accepted practice and I am sure that it is a very sound scheme. A large proportion of today's school leavers go to Australia; my destination was Africa, East Africa to be exact and Kenya Colony, as it was then known, to be absolutely precise. My father had always had a dream of owning a farm or a little land in that beautiful country, from before the First World War. In about 1921, he bought some land on the slopes of Mount Elgon, on the plain below and around the small village of Kitale. He was advised against the purchase of the farm on the slopes of the mountain, later to be called Chorlim, by the experts. My father may not have been an expert, but he was extremely knowledgeable. He was aware that Mount Elgon had been a volcano and that old lava is the most productive soil, so Chorlim became the best of our many farms in Kenya, probably one of the best in the whole country and, certainly to my eyes, the most beautiful.

One talks about buying a farm, but the land was then virgin forest and had to be totally cleared before any form of ploughing could take place. The forest behind Chorlim was, and still is, full of elephants and buffalo and over the years the former

64

The Author as a young blade

The Author with his sisters
Bronwen and Elizabeth in
September 1917

(*Left*) The Author's fa
with one of his daught

(*Below*) Chirk Castle |
Philip Wilson Steer

(*Right*) A performanc
The Reluctant Dragor
Chirk, the Author in
armour, with his twin
sister Bronwen

(*Lower right*) Interior
Chirk, by Sir John La
Notice the Author's
stringless tennis racke

The Author's mother with
her children

A view from Eilan Shona i
Loch Moidart on the west
coast of Scotland

The Author with his first
wife Nucci, at the time of
their marriage

The house at Chorlim
Kenya built by the
author's father in the
20s

(*Left*) Nucci with her hair down

(*Below*) In the Alvis Speed 20 in Spain

(*Right*) A briefing on exercise during the War

(*Lower right*) An exhausting dinner in Santos, Brazil, after the War

The Author's younger daughters Jessica and Camilla
at Mas Palomas, Las Palmas

In America, 1957. President Eisenhower laughs
at John Shapiro's joke

The Author with his second wife Gillie

Avington Manor on the Kennet near Hungerford

(*Above*) A trompe l'oeil painting of Thornton Stud in Yorkshire by Graham Rust

(*Below*) The Author with his trainer Henry Cecil and Derby winner Slip Anchor in 1985

(*Right*) Four daughters: (from l to r) Susie Buchan, Hazel Czernin, Jessica White and Camilla Acloque

(*Lower right*) Eighteen grandchildren

A caricature by Cad of a powerful combination:
Henry Cecil, Lester Piggott, and the Author

were always a danger, not to the human beings so much as to the crops. An elephant in a maize shamba did untold damage, as can be well imagined. Fortunately for later generations and the present African owners, a great deal of trouble was taken in this clearing operation.

Most of the houses had large and beautiful trees on the lawns around them, and were very similar to the better type of English country house. This is not surprising as quite a large number of the original settlers came from upper-class families and tried, mostly successfully, to reproduce what they had been used to in their childhood. Among these were Lord Francis Scott, Lord Delamere, Mervyn Ridley and many others including my father who, however, was not a permanent resident in the country and therefore less well-known than the rest.

It was one of my father's visits in the early 1920s that he made friends with the celebrated Ewart Grogan. Grogan owned a lot of things in Kenya and had actually settled in the country after his walk from the Cape to Cairo in 1897. He had lived with cannibals and many splendid stories are told of this very ebullient, Irish character. When he was electioneering in Kenya, on one occasion he was being heckled by the local Africans. His reply to them was, 'I've eaten you lot, pickled, and you are nasty.' This was greeted with loud applause, because his audience knew it to be at least partly true. My father and Grogan became partners, which was not a good idea and lasted a very short time. There was never any animosity between them, but Grogan was the sort of man who was on top of the world one moment and broke the next. The long and short of their parting was that my Father found himself with much more land, including the whole ridge above Nakuru as well as Elburgon, and Molo, and various other things such as shares in a newspaper. He had to either cut his losses or try and make a go in the country. He decided on the latter course and so our association with Kenya began. The newspaper shares became a controlling interest in the *East African Standard*, which was the major newspaper in the colony, and of course the new land had to be managed. My father soon found out that the biggest danger was dishonesty. An owner who, when there were no telephones, could only reach you at a pinch in three weeks, was a sitting duck. He decided to ask a young cousin of ours, Buster Powles, who was then in the Army of Occupation in Cologne, if he would like to take the chance and go out to Kenya. Luckily for our family he agreed and eventually became in charge of everything, a job which he carried out with great success and total integrity until Kenyan Independence in 1963.

So, I was to sail to Kenya with my father and go on a safari, after a little practice with a rifle and the acquisition of the regulation clothes, including mosquito boots and a topee. It was early days and the sun was regarded as a great danger, which it isn't, but the mosquitos were still very prevalent, bringing malaria and blackwater fever. Nowadays they are very largely under control and the hated mosquito net is something of the past.

The train ambled gaily through the centre of France to Marseilles, that city associated with crime and bouillabaisse. I certainly had the most marvellous dish of the latter, but crime I was protected from, during the one night we spent before boarding a German ship, the SS *Naivasha*. Shy and introverted, all of a sudden I stepped into a world, new and quite unknown. I remember my father telling me to study the people wandering about and try to place them, as there were always certain types on every voyage: the drunk, the games organiser, the ship's minx and the bore, etc. They were all there, but I don't think I spotted them very quickly. The drunk was easily discerned for the simple reason that he was unconscious and all the bars were closed to him. His name was Greswald Williams and I discovered later that he was, or rather had been, a butcher in, I think, Birmingham. He had clearly prospered and

had a nice property and a house at the foot of the escarpment between Nairobi and Naivasha. Among the amazing
assortment of men and women on board, quite a number
appeared to be, or said they were, guests of Mr Williams.
When this gentleman came round from his really monumental
hangover, he was very surprised to see this motley gathering,
as he had no recollection of inviting them. However, he had a
curious little secretary who assured him that he had done so
and in any case there was no going back halfway through the
Mediterranean. One lady not in that party, called Priscilla, had
been back to England to have her baby, it being thought far
too dangerous to give birth in such an outlandish place as
Kenya in those days. I used to help her push the pram up and
down the deck and needless to say, listen to her life story on
the top deck in the balmy evenings, or possibly when watching
the phosphorescence from the stern. I suppose it was here that
I discovered that people were apt to load their troubles on my
inadequate shoulders. Anyway, they have continued to do so
over the years. Perhaps I encouraged it a little: maybe it's the
dormant writer in me!

Priscilla was married to a small and fiery-tempered man, she
told me, and she didn't seem to think that her marriage would
last very long. In this she was completely correct. When we
eventually arrived in Nairobi I was anxious to see this gentleman, and was not disappointed. He was like an angry ferret
and that very evening had a tremendous fight in the Muthaiga
Club that I witnessed. He ended up beneath a stuffed lion in a
glass cage; the lion is still there sixty years later. They were
divorced quite soon and he married again, but was killed with
his bride in a small plane on their honeymoon. It was
rumoured that he had had a bullet in his head. Anything, and
everything, was possible in Kenya in those days.

One of the passengers, on the good ship *Naivasha*, also a
guest of Mr Williams, had only one leg, and was said to write a
gossip column. One evening I happened to be on the top deck

behind the funnel, when I overheard the following conversation.

'If it wasn't for the fact that you had a wooden leg I would knock you out here and now.' 'Well, you haven't a wooden leg', came the reply, together with a well-timed right hook. Mr William's secretary was carried to bed, out for the count.

Another of these new friends was a 'Mannequin' (they would call her a model today). She claimed to work in Sloane Street, which has always puzzled me. Perhaps she was referring to some other work that I didn't know about then. I shall certainly never know now.

The ship put in at Beirut and I was taken to see Baalbek, which sadly, I have never been able to revisit. Then came the first glimpse of Port Said. It used to be said that if one sat in the hall of Simon Artz, the big shop in Port Said, you might eventually meet all the people you knew. I suppose the equivalent today would be the departure lounge at Heathrow, not nearly so romantic and the coffee was a lot better in Simon Artz. The Galli Galli man was a great feature at Port Said and, as I have always had a penchant for conjurers, he was just up my street and I revelled in his discovering numbers of little live chicks in all my pockets.

The arrival in Mombasa I remember as being scented with the aroma of frangipani, which has remained a favourite all my life. The journey on the winding railway to Nairobi was exciting. A few years later I took this trip with Nucci and she insisted on looking for lions; needless to say in the early morning, no doubt on the Kapiti Plains, there stood a large black-maned lion staring at us as we slowly chugged by. I was not allowed to forget this. Game parks were not thought of in those days when the White Hunter was the silent hero.

The White Hunter that we went with was, in fact, called 'Hunter' and became, or already was, renowned. He was a quiet, efficient man who produced what was wanted and knew the animal world inside out. Thee was one thing about him I never liked, though I might be doing him an injustice. I think that he liked, or enjoyed to kill. He was employed to cull the lion population in the Serengeti, which was no doubt necessary for the good of the breed, but he seemed rather to relish the numbers he slaughtered.

We went down past Narok to the Mara river and it took a long time crossing dried river beds. Once we were watching a slow trickle coming round the corner, yet ten minutes later were being cut off by a roaring torrent. I used to walk gently about in the evenings with a .22 rifle trying to shoot a bustard in the head for dinner, where today the tour leaders call upon their myriad passengers to get back in their mini buses before they are attacked by the furious beasts lurking in the bushes. It is easy to be sarcastic when one has seen something unspoilt. I don't doubt that those people who used to shoot snipe in Belgrave Square would have a few things to say today. I enjoyed the safari hugely, with distinct spasms of home sickness, and quiet times spent desperately trying to write poetry. A wild desire to get the change of rhythm in the eighth line of an ode was my passion at the time.

On the way back to our farm at Chorlim, I had been asked to stay the night with Mr Williams at his house at the bottom of the escarpment. This I did with a certain amount of trepidation and for once I was right in being a little nervous. After the quiet tented life in the Mara River area it was a distinct shock, at my tender age, to be greeted by a very English butler at the door with, 'Good evening, Sir. And who will you be sleeping with tonight?' I have spent the years since wondering what a really good answer could have been. Perhaps, 'Please show me the "menu".' All I remember of the visit was some poor man being lured into the idea of shooting a leopard and, after hours of stalking, being shown the beast lurking under a bush not far from the house. He fired two shots into what turned out to be a stuffed rug, especially placed there for his benefit. I suppose it was meant to deflate his ego and it probably did.

Another typical Kenyan story comes to mind from after the War, when Tom Harcourt Powell, who was working for us then, and I decided to go out and see how things were going. We set off to Kisumu in a propeller-driven Constellation, which flew much lower than the jets of today. It was rather bumpy and we joined up with a lady called Helen who had been a bridesmaid at my wedding, and whose husband was in charge of a big tea plantation at Kericho. He was a very temperamental fellow and I don't think the marriage was going very well. We drove to Kericho where there was a party going on. Helen's husband asked me to come with him on the drive back to his place, where we were all staying. He suddenly diverted and drove off into a sort of forest. I suppose I assumed it was a short cut until he stopped the car, turned out the lights, took a revolver out of his pocket and placed in on the seat between us. All I remember thinking was, 'So, we're back in Kenya!' He didn't threaten me but suggested that Tom was paying too much attention to Helen. We went on quite amicably but I was not sorry to leave the next day.

Helen, Tom and I stopped for a picnic somewhere on our way to Chorlim on the slopes of Mount Elgon. I thought that Tom was perhaps getting a little bit too keen and Helen told us all her woes and the tribulations of her marriage. As the afternoon wore on, I was tiring of all the emotion and began to wonder whether the 'Happy Valley' crowd's excuse for their behaviour – the 'altitude' – might not have a little truth in it. Eventually we came to Eldoret and decided to stay the night there. It was a pleasant little town and I was pleased to go to bed. However, I was rudely awakened by the sound of bagpipes. I thought I really had gone mad but it turned out to be St Andrew's Day and all the local Scots were celebrating. That was the end of that evening's sleep. We dropped Helen off somewhere and went about our business on the farms until the time came to leave to go back from Kisumu. We were waiting to board the plane when I was called to the telephone. It was our friend in Kericho who said he was setting off with a horse whip to deal with us. I was not very disturbed for although Kericho was not all that far, the road was very steep and anyway I could see our plane with the engines running; we escaped the horsewhip very easily.

We used to plough with oxen on my father's Kenyan farms before the War and I can remember boasting in later years that we were the biggest owners of working oxen in the world. Actually, it was almost certainly true. The sight of sixteen ploughs, each one pulled by sixteen oxen, that is to say, 176 splendid beasts in one field, is something I shall never forget, and they were very efficient too. The reason for doing this was partly because we had the space to breed, but really because petrol became more expensive the further inland you were situated, and we were nearly on the borders of Uganda.

The main crop on all the farms was maize, but we did grow a fair amount of wheat, which thrived at certain altitudes. A small quantity of coffee was grown at Chorlim, although it was really too high up and couldn't compete with the better results obtained near Nairobi. I can remember going to see a farm which we were thinking of buying where they were growing sisal, but I don't think we ever grew it ourselves. We had fairly large numbers of cattle and over the years we imported bulls from England to improve the breed. Some were successful and others not, but on the whole it was better to maintain a connection with the local breed and use the attractive humped Boran bulls.

When Independence came it was decided that we should get out altogether and sell the farms. It was obvious that absentee landlords were not going to be popular with the new regime. We were fairly lucky as the farms on the slopes of Mount Elgon – Chorlim, Sabwani and 66 – were taken over by the government and still are owned by them. They kept our managers on. Some of the other farms were bought by locals, which could be awkward as they arrived with cash and the transactions thereafter were long and laborious. One couldn't export Kenya shillings and, while these transactions were going on, the farms continued to make profits, accumulating large sums. We thought the best thing to do would be to invest in something that we could eventually be bought out of in a negotiable currency. We therefore started to buy up small hotels and suchlike. These we sold out to the Block group eventually, who owned most of the big hotels already and were able to pay in sterling.

The newspapers were a different story. At the time of Independence we were publishing the *East African Standard* and various local-language papers, as well as the *Uganda Argus* and the local paper of Tanzania. Over and above this the printing works used to print *Time* magazine and various similar journals. It was difficult to get management and the local Africans had not reached the necessary standards. Eventually the whole business was taken over by Lonrho and Tiny Rowland. He may not be very popular in the City of London, but I look upon him in quite a different way and I am glad to say that recently he told me that the enterprise was flourishing.

CHAPTER SEVEN

Visitors to Chirk

D URING MY DAYS AT ETON, ENCOURAGED BY MY
father, I had read a book called *An Experiment with
Time* by J. W. Dunne. Mr Dunne had, I believe, been
one of those men – my father was another – who tried to build
and fly an aeroplane at exactly the same time that the Wright
Brothers succeeded in their attempts. I have a picture of my
father's efforts; the aeroplane looks very frail, but clearly some
of my father's ideas were correct. Whether this link with
Dunne persuaded my father to read his views on Time, I don't
know, but he was very fascinated with them, and so was I.
Although it is a very tiring process, it is possible, with the aid
of a pencil and paper under the pillow, to put down sufficient
during the night to recall in the morning what one has dreamt.
One learns to scribble a few words when one is still almost
asleep. In very simple terms Dunne's theory was that one's
clock-conscious way of thinking ceases when one is asleep and
one slips into another sort of time, when the past and future
get mixed. Therefore, if one can eliminate the bits that are past
it is possible to foresee some of the future. Dunne gives a lot of
examples where the main facts may be correct, but the details
are wrong.

I had an early success, if that is the correct word, when I
dreamt that I saw my sister's young governess riding over the
jumps in the park at Chirk and then falling and being knocked
unconscious. Two days later this lady tripped down the stairs
at Chirk and suffered concussion. Coincidence if you like, but I
was hooked and have been ever since. Nowadays there are

innumerable books on the subject and Dunne is considered very out of date, but he set me off on an unending exploration, which I did not expect to show results, but which I find absorbing. I quietly waded through Ouspensky and at Cambridge decided that I would study Freud on Dreams. One night I had a very vivid dream which showed the whole British Navy in some harbour and a mass of other ships of all kinds and sorts. When I woke up I rushed off to Freud to see what this might signify. To my slight horror the master averred that ships represented women. As I was 19 at the time I dare say he was correct on that occasion.

Although I have been a very mild and amateurish student of what is called the 'occult', it is encouraging to me that after all these years even the most bigoted scientists are agreeing that such things as ESP exist and, although nobody knows what it is, at least it is accepted that there is something. I was once staying with some friends in Essex and amongst the guests was a charming old Admiral who was deeply interested in the psychic world and all such kindred subjects. He asked me one evening to do a mild experiment with the throwing of dice and I was happy to oblige as he was an interesting man. He made me throw two dice against a cushion, from which they could bounce off, to obviate any possible twists or try-ons. He asked me first to throw high and for about twenty throws or more I never threw less than four and frequently double sixes. Then he said, 'Now throw low.' I started off with double ones and continued in much the same vein. The Admiral was really keen for me to become a guinea pig in a laboratory test but I declined. I don't really know why I refused but I never had any real inclination to get personally involved in these matters. When I was quite small I used to be able to throw a pack of cards on the floor face down, or let somebody else do it, and then pick out the four aces. I claim absolutely no strange powers but probably I had, or even have, this ESP slightly higher than others.

Another book, which probably interested me most of those which I read in my youth, was again suggested to me by my father. It was Oswald Spengler's *Decline of the West*. Why on earth my father should have thought that someone of 18 or 19, unless he were quite amazingly erudite, could possibly understand such a work, I shall never understand. However, I understood enough to believe that basically his theory of cultures, and how they have their Spring, Summer, Autumn and Winter, is correct. I cannot possibly argue his details, which have been torn to shreds by many great men and some very eminent historians, and no doubt such a book is full of errors; however, it is still possible that he is correct in general. He has one fan left in the world at any rate. My father-in-law used to know Spengler and, being a very cultivated and knowledgeable man himself, spent many evenings discussing matters with him and another philosopher friend called Count Keyserling. My father-in-law always told me that Spengler was interesting but completely stubborn and pig-headed and found it almost impossible to admit that there was another point of view. Anyone who has read his masterpiece will agree that the tone is confident, dictatorial and distinctly arrogant. I am extremely grateful that I at least toyed with these works at an early age.

I used even to show off at Cambridge by slipping into some essay or other such comments as, 'of course, Spengler takes a different view'. One day my tutor sent for me and said, 'Who is this Spengler? I've never read him and I can't find anyone else who has. Perhaps you had better read a paper to the College on this work.' So it is, one is brought down to earth. Trying to make a precis of Spengler's introduction , which is at least one hundred pages long, is something I would not care to repeat, and I doubt whether anybody was the wiser after my nervous oration.

Two other events in my early youth stand out as having some effect on me in later years and they both took place whilst I was at Summerfields. I cannot imagine who was

75

responsible in that very strict preparatory school for suggest-
ing that the boys would be interested in listening to a certain
M. Coué. I don't suppose there are too many people who
remember Coué today, but at that time, in the early 1920s, he
was quite well known. He was a psychological healer whose
basic tenet was that you could influence yourself and your
achievements by repeating certain ritual homilies so many
times. Thus, his 'every day in every way I am getting better and
better', was supposed to help the sick. Presumably he was only
advocating that the mind influences the body, which every self-
respecting medical man must accept today. Perhaps they didn't
then. I remember being impressed by this little man with a
foreign accent and I thank the school for an original idea. The
second incident was a visit from a conjuror who specialised in
such tricks as tying a knot in a handkerchief with one flick and
then showing in slow motion how it was done. It takes a lot of
practice but I can still do it, and a few others; I wish I had
practised more.

In the holidays, amongst the many guests who used to come
and stay, was Hilaire Belloc. He was always dressed in black
with elastic-sided boots. As he had rather a florid complexion
and sideburns, he was frequently taken for the butler when
there was a party, which for some mysterious reason delighted
him. He used to teach me all sorts of tricks with paper, most of
which I can still do today, such as making a bird which flaps its
wings when you pull its tail. Also, he used to be able to prove
Pythagoras's Theorem – the one that says that 'the square on
the hypotenuse of a right-angled triangle is equal to the sum of
the squares on the other two sides' – by cutting out two tri-
angles and putting them onto a piece of paper in a particular
way. While I remember how to do this, I am sad to have
forgotten his absolute proof of the Trinity, which he demonstrated in a somewhat similar fashion!

One day he arrived in a battered Ford motor car, driven by
Elizabeth Herbert, a charming American lady, who spent a lot

of her time looking after this remarkable man. In the back of the car were rows of bottles laid out in straw, like a miniature wine cellar, which is indeed what it was. He is the only person whom I have ever known who used to go to bed, gently walking across the courtyard at Chirk, with a bottle of port under each arm, and then drink them. On this occasion, on arrival, he asked for the use of a room with a large table and slightly ungraciously was given the Billiard room. He also asked for an inordinate amount – reams, or bushels – of tissue paper. He worked steadily for several days and none of us could make out what he was up to, including my parents. He then asked whether he could build a fire in the middle of the courtyard and this again was permitted. Eventually he emerged with a vast balloon made of the tissue paper and by placing it, somehow, above his fire without burning it, filled it with hot air so that it rose slowly above the battlements. He then proceeded to chase it across Wales in the dilapidated Ford, until its final disappearance, or demise. He had his famous political and unpublished poems privately printed in Oswestry for my father's birthday. I have them still and they are probably unique.

Other people of mark whom we children got to know were sometimes less attractive, or perhaps they were totally uninterested in us. The first time I came across Augustus John, he was lying, quite drunk, on one of the benches in the garden at Chirk. Bronwen and I were rather alarmed at this bearded figure but became more accustomed to him as time went on. George Moore was always rather preoccupied. One day (my father told me) in London he came shuffling over from Ebury Street with a great problem that he couldn't solve. 'I keep on writing down', he said to my father, '"she was in the habit of wearing a habit", and it isn't right and I can't think how to alter it.' Gently my father murmured, 'What about, "she was used to wearing a habit"?' 'Ah, yes, yes, many thanks.' Then he departed back to Ebury Street. Bronwen and I had both been painted by a young man called Naviasky, after we had performed in a pageant in Harlech Castle with my parents. My portrait is as the young Prince Edward in red velvet and in Bronwen's she is wearing a green and white halved top piece. George Moore had arrived and my father showed him the pictures; he was quite unaware that the young Naviasky was among the guests. After some pondering the great man said, 'Yes, very slick, the sort of thing a young Jew would do.' The silence lasted quite a long time.

One of the more remarkable people who came often was a certain Hugo Rumbold. His brother was the well-known Ambassador, Sir Horace, and I imagine Hugo was the black sheep of the family. He stuttered quite badly but when he was dressed up as a lady, which was his forte, this stutter vanished altogether. I can well remember as a child, my mother bringing this exotic creature to see us before they went down to dinner. He invariably fooled all the guests and the only lapse occurred, I believe, when once he hesitated over the offer of a glass of port. The ladies used to unburden their womanly worries to him and were far from pleased when the eventual denouement took place. He was able to fool the same people both at Chirk and, in the same week, again in London. He died in a dentist's chair in Arizona, which seems in keeping with his rather exotic life style.

There was a splendid man called Sir John Bland Sutton who was a leading surgeon and had risen to his position from cleaning the corridors of the Middlesex Hospital, a really amazing performance. He had a rather formidable wife who was, I suppose, of slightly better breeding. She used to keep a strict eye during lunch when we children practically fought to sit next to him. One day he was educating one of my sisters on the subject of the menstruation of elephants when he was stopped – 'that will be enough, John' – from the other side of the table. On another occasion, when he was leaving and being seen off by all the house party, an old aunt of ours called Great

Aunt Jane rather unwisely said, 'Tell us, Sir John, what is your favourite operation?' With no hesitation at all came the reply, 'Circumcision, dear lady', with which he left.

When Rudyard Kipling came to stay, it was an event because he was practically revered by my father and also by me in a small way. He came to my room and offered to sign the whole collection of his works which I had in the red leather pocket edition. However, we were interrupted by his wife, Carrie, who refused to let him sign. She was very protective and tiresome and irritated my father by always joining them when they were out for a walk. Bronwen and I were aware that Kipling had two phobias: firstly, Germans (his son had been killed in the War) and secondly, aeroplanes, as he always maintained they were trying to knock down his chimneys. One day he, Bronwen and I were strolling in the garden and talking of these things. I was inspired to ask him if he would travel in an airship. 'What! Locked in a silver coffin with a lot of Boche?' was his instant reply. I took him to the sheepdog trials that used to take place at Vivod (the home of the Bests) near Llangollen. He was a master at getting the shepherds to talk and explain all about the trials and their lives. He promised me he would write a story about them, but sadly he never got round to it.

Other very regular and welcome visitors to Chirk were Gonda and Charmian, the two daughters of my mother's brother Nony and his wife, Iris Graham. She deserted them early on and they were more or less brought up by unsatisfactory stepmothers, but mostly by my mother. They were two extra sisters as far as I was concerned. Gonda (I think she was called Gonda because her father had a Lagonda motor car at the time, but I could be wrong) was dark and very good looking with wonderful teeth. She was a sort of gypsy at heart and when she came to Chirk, used to camp out on the moors and come over to the castle to eat. One day she lit a fire in the courtyard and was found roasting a mouse. To everybody's surprise Gonda married a doctor called Morrison who had a practice near Leicester and ran a pack of basset hounds. When Nucci and I visited her once, she was dressed in blue shorts with any amount of daggers and dirks sticking out of everywhere. Her sister Charmain was much more conventional, but was also very pretty. She married and had two children, but is now a widow and remains one of my really great friends.

But of all the people who came down often to Chirk, the most popular, even with my father, was Aunt Poots. My mother's sister was totally unlike my mother in every way, but they always remained friends. She played the piano by ear and repeated anything she heard straight away with all the frills. She had first married Noel Francis, a good-looking and attractive fellow, who later took to the bottle. I was a page at their wedding in 1916. At Chirk, when everyone went to bed, we used to repair to Poot's bedroom in which there was a grand piano and sing away into the night. She later married Humphrey Butler who was at one time or another equerry to Prince George, Duke of Kent, and to George, the King of Greece, who lived in London for many years. She lived in Connaught Square and kept 'open house': that is to say anyone could walk in around 6 pm and find a lot of friends, usually with someone playing the piano (quite often Hutch). Friends included Noel Coward, Philip Astley and the Prince of Wales – the Duke of Windsor to be. I remember her saying to me, when I was about fifteen, 'You see that little man there who looks like a jockey. Go and be nice to him.' He was in fact, Lord Rootes.

Poots took me to a night club for the first time. I think it was called the Kit Kat and the Cabaret artist decided she would sing her songs with her arm around my reddened neck. She was a nice lady called Sophie Tucker. On another evening at Connaught Square, the telephone rang and as usual Poots answered it sitting on the floor in the middle of all her guests. She said, 'Darlings – do shut up – it's the King', and it probably was.

CHAPTER EIGHT

Spain and Sister Priscilla

I HAVE ALREADY DESCRIBED THE KENYAN AND Munich episodes that filled most of my gap between Eton and Cambridge. My mother also arranged a theatrical interlude, taking us to the Passion Play at Oberammergau. We stayed with a young carpenter who was playing the part of Christ and we were all duly impressed by the serenity of the performance. Poor Judas got very few people to stay with him and I sincerely hope his village friends made it up to him afterwards. The performance lasted about eight hours with a longish interval for lunch. When the story was approaching the crucifixion, there was a loud and real thunderclap and rain fell heavily on the open stage. It was extremely dramatic, until an American lady sitting some rows in front of us suddenly stood up and shouted, 'They're gonna kill him, they're gonna kill him'; one vulture had surely missed its culture.

I am afraid that my time at Cambridge was far from being devoted solely to the scholarly and uplifting and my playgoing continued there. One of my favourite ways of spending an evening was at the Cambridge Festival Theatre, where there was a succession of new touring companies, almost always good ones. A number of actresses who performed there in my day went on to fame and fortune: Flora Robson, Jessica Tandy, and Margaret Rawlings were among them. My best friend was Robert Matthew, who was a little older than myself, but had been at the same house at Eton. He later became a barrister and a Member of Parliament, but died in his fifties. One evening Bob and I arrived slightly late and

walked into the auditorium as quietly as we could. A woman
was speaking and I was suddenly rooted to the spot. It was
Margaret Rawlings, and if ever it can be said that someone fell
in love with a voice, it was at that moment. I do not suppose
that I was the only one on whom she had this exciting effect,
but it is something I remember vividly to this day. In the
restaurant attached to the theatre were two waitresses, named
Doris and Dot. They were dressed in green trouser suits and
the table cloths were black. With large cigars protruding from
our lips Bob and I thought that life had nothing better to offer.
Perhaps we were right.

Bob and I decided that, in the long vacation, we should visit
Spain and see the famous Fiesta de San Firmin at Pamplona.
Spain had not yet been discovered by the British in those far-
off days and we were the only British present in Pamplona.
The bands started off from the main square at about
12 o'clock in the morning, all playing different tunes, and the
Fiesta was on. Domingo Ortega was the fashionable bull-
fighter of the day, although we were fortunate enough to see
Belmonte as well, no doubt in his later years, but a legend then
and for always. At the first bullfight we attended, we were
much taken by some beautiful ladies all dressed up to the
nines. They were in two boxes with very exotic shawls dis-
played hanging down over the sides. After the corrida, we
thought that it would be worthwhile trying to make their
acquaintance, although we were pretty certain they were very
grand princesses or contessas. It was a slight shock to be loudly
laughed at and informed that they were showgirls advertising
the local brothel.

Outside the bullring a procession was starting up, consisting
of a series of huge figures carried by men strapped-in under-
neath. We followed for a bit and noticed that after a few
blocks, the procession halted and everyone repaired to the
local bar to imbibe vast quantities of red wine. Bob and I, no
doubt encouraged by the vino, got under two of the large

figures and marched off, swaying merrily down the street. When the others came out of the bar and discovered we were English and couldn't speak Spanish, instead of being annoyed they insisted that we continue to join in all their festivities.

It was a period in Spanish history when the King was either about to be thrown out, or already had been, and it was perhaps a little awkward that our only Spanish seemed to consist of 'Viva el Rey'. As night fell, we thought we had better go to sleep, but this was strictly forbidden by our new friends and any attempt was immediately frustrated by the bands playing under our windows. This went on for three nights until, totally exhausted, we strode out of the town and lay down in the middle of the Navarra plains where we slept long and deep till kicked awake by a bearded shepherd. Apart from proving satisfactorily that it was possible to fry eggs on the pavement in a heatwave on the Puerto del Sol in Madrid, I remember little else of that trip, which may be as well.

My parents had some very old and good Spanish friends, the Infante and Infanta D'Orleans Bourbon, Prince Ali and Princess Bea to all of us. She was my godmother and a daughter of Queen Victoria's son, The Duke of Edinburgh, and consequently a sister of Queen Marie of Rumania and the Grand Duchess Kyril of Russia. She was totally charming and very proud of being, as she called it, a 'Breetish Princess'. She spoke all her languages with a strong foreign accent. Prince Ali, who was a cousin of the Spanish King, Alfonso XIII, was a really remarkable man of immense character. It was his ambition to show that royalty, far from being effete, were just as capable of being successful in almost any field as any ordinary person. When the royal family were obliged to leave Spain in the early 1930s, Prince Ali settled his family in Switzerland and, having very little money, took a job on the factory floor at Fords in Paris, under the assumed name of Mr Orleans. By dint of hard work and study he struck lucky. One day his immediate boss came in and said, 'Does anyone here speak Spanish?' Of course

Prince Ali stuck his hand up. He found himself being sent to do a job in Spain where he had to disguise himself as a German, so as not to be recognised. By sheer ability, he rose to become the European Representative of the company and his alias was only broken when he had to face Mr Ford himself, in the USA, whom he had met in the past on several occasions and had had as a guest in Spain.

On the next trip made by Bob and myself to Spain, Prince Ali asked me if I would be good enough to visit his old home at San Lucar de Barrameda and see if all was well. This we did and a very strange experience it was. We had introductions to a Senor Garcia, who was looking after the Palace in San Lucar and also to the Marquis of Torre Soto, the head of the Gonzalez family in Jerez. We arrived eventually by car in San Lucar and Senor Garcia took us to the Palace. We were told to stay there and that there would be a dinner party for us in the evening. The rooms still had the names of the last occupants on them, such as the Queen of Rumania. When the time came for dinner Bob and I, dressed we hoped reasonably smartly, started to walk down the stairs to the patio. We were astonished to be met by a vast cohort of people who were determined to shake our hands and entertain us to the full. How we got through that immense dinner (I even made a speech in Spanish) I shall never know. All I do remember was that my neighbour's sole contribution in English was, 'You lika the pork meat, yes?'

Moving on to Jerez, we duly formed up to see the Marquis de Torre Soto, who turned out to be a man of immense age. He opened the conversation by waving his arms at a number of huge photographs all round the room and saying, 'Those are my eleven sons and now we will go down to the polo ground'. The family were delightful and I was entranced that the sherry decanter in their house had 'sherry' written on it in English. I was not so aware then of the great English connection and of how many English ladies have married into those famous Jerez families. In the evening we all got rather merry with some of the sons and their friends. One of the merriest, and most attractive, was José Antonio, later more or less sanctified by Franco. His name was given to one of the main Avenidas in Madrid, and to streets in many other cities throughout the country. He was killed in the Spanish Civil War.

With the outbreak of the Spanish Civil War, my sister Priscilla, usually known as Pip, started showing a great desire to take part in some sort of action. When she was small we used to call her 'Chatterbox' and she sat in her high chair talking away whether anyone was listening, or understood, or not. She was of a cheerful and jolly disposition, one of the world's great optimists. Prince Ali had become Head of the Airforce under General Franco and his three sons, Alvaro, Alonso and Ataulfo were all playing their part. It was the fashion at that time to take very strong sides in this conflict and the vast majority of those who went to give their help gave it to the Russian-backed Republican side. I am glad to say that Pip chose otherwise, not only because it was the winning side, but with hindsight General Franco's victory gave Spain at least thirty years of peace, which had been unknown for a long time in that lovely country. Also, when the Hitler war broke out three years later and we had our backs very much to the wall, at no time did the Spanish allow Germany or Italy to use their country, despite what Hitler, or Mussolini, had done to help General Franco in his war. This cannot have been easy and I think it should not be forgotten.

This particular civil war was no exception to the usual pattern of civil wars: it was exceedingly cruel and unpleasant. Why my parents allowed Pip to go out there as an inexperienced nurse at the age of 18, I shall never quite understand. After some time my mother started to get agitated, despite the fact that Pip would clearly be looked after, or at least kept an eye on, by Prince Ali, and particularly by Princess Bea. One day my mother suggested to me that as I had been to Spain, even though my Spanish was virtually non-existent I might care to go out to the war and see if I could find Pip and discover exactly what she was up to. Why I should have agreed to do this, let alone why Nucci agreed, I cannot even remember. However, armed with something very important-looking written in green ink in my passport by the Foreign Office, I set off towards Hendaye and Irun.

Strange though it may seem now, the task of finding one English girl was not as difficult as it sounds. There was an extraordinary camaraderie and the fact that there was only a handful of English girl supporters made it easier. Ordinary soldiers had actually heard of an English girl called Pip. I was told that the best thing to do was to go to the city where the headquarters was and work from there. At that time it was Zaragoza and there I went without too much difficulty, aided by a driver called Jesus, who appeared from somewhere. At that time I had never seen or had anything to do with war and was still in my early 20s, so I was duly impressed by the sandbags and general feeling of activity. I repaired to the main hotel and decided that probably the best place to be was the bar, certainly not to drink the totally horrible local whisky, but in the hope that someone would come in who might be able to help. This turned out to be an excellent decision and before long in walked a Catholic priest whom I had known slightly in London, followed by another young man, disguised as a Spanish Foreign Legionnaire, who had been to stay at Chirk.

It transpired that Pip was at that moment very busy in the Battle of Teruel. I don't think that my parents had visualised anything more than her being in some base camp, helping a bit with bandages. Instead, owing to the enormous shortages of everything, she found herself in the front line dealing with every kind of nastiness and injecting people in the heart, for instance, when she had no experience or training whatsoever. Whilst waiting for this battle to come to its conclusion, I was taken to the Front Line by my new-found friends, but with no great enthusiasm on my part. I do, however, remember passing a huge compound of prisoners and averting my head very rapidly when I realised that they were all speaking English, or should I say Scots. A few days later, Ataulfo appeared in charge of a squadron of bombers who used to go and drop their wares on Barcelona. His pilots were all young Germans doing a six-month stint. I used to have dinner with them in the hotel, when these young boys showed me their palms and asked what I thought their future held. Whether Ataulfo put them up to this, I do not know, but I did my best to alleviate their forebodings and in return they used to fly low over the hotel to wake me in time for breakfast. This was the first, but not the last, time I heard the roaring engines of Heinkel Bombers.

When I left Spain I went straight to Munich, where Nucci was visiting her family. I stayed at Schloss Niederarnbach with my sister-in-law Malies, Nucci's eldest sister, and her husband Max. We got on extremely well together, but I remember vividly saying quite casually to Max, 'I saw some of your young pilots three nights ago in Spain.'

'There are no Germans in Spain', came the reply.

'Don't be silly', I said, 'I spoke to them, I can give you names if you like.'

'There are no Germans fighting in Spain, the Führer has said so!'

'Now at least I understood the meaning of propaganda and the skill and cunning of Dr Goebbels. I remained silent and distinctly apprehensive. Six months later Max was praising the daring and skill of the pilots in Spain. The Führer had said so.

Pip continued her very gallant and strenuous career with the Franco forces and was highly commended, and decorated, by the General for her efforts. In due course she flew over Madrid in the victory parade. In 1939, convinced that her experience would be invaluable, she immediately volunteered for service overseas and was shocked when our authorities suggested a job as a V.A.D. in the country would be more suitable. Not so for my sister. She went to the French and soon found herself somewhere in the Maginot Line area awaiting events. When they eventually came, like a good many others, she found herself being hotly pursued across France and was lucky to get on board a ship full of Poles in Bordeaux. She arrived in London with little more than a nightdress and a wild desire to help the Poles.

Somehow she managed to get to know General Sikorski and in no time at all she was running hospitals in Scotland for the Poles, apparently with great success. I once met her quite by chance on a train somewhere in England. She was wearing a Polish uniform with Spanish medals. I warned her that she might get shot but of course nothing happened. At that time, certainly in London, you could have walked about covered in swastikas and nobody would have said a thing, as there was such a variety of people and armies in the country.

A number of Poles who had managed to escape across Europe had been detained in Spain and the Polish authorities in England wanted them released. Although ostensibly Pip went to Spain to visit the British Consulate in Barcelona, I'm sure that her close ties with Spain and the Poles, and her speaking both languages, must have been used to help the detained Poles get out of the country and join their fellow-countrymen in Scotland.

It was during this period that she fell in love with a Spaniard called José Luis de Vilallonga and married him in Spain. They came over to England at the end of the war, on their way to make their home in the Argentine. She asked me whether I could arrange a berth on one of our ships. I pointed out to her that she appeared to be very pregnant. She said that was not a problem, but I managed to find two doctors who needed a holiday (one of them, in fact, was a dentist), and they all set sail for Buenos Aires via Las Palmas and Rio de Janeiro. Our stewards on the boat were Chinese and they, together with the doctors, helped Pip to produce a son shortly before arriving at Las Palmas.

Pip and José Luis lived in Buenos Aires for about three or four years and she started a dress shop. I don't think it was a great success and the marriage was heading for the rocks. My father had left his studio in Cadogan Lane to Priscilla and for a time José Luis took up residence there with a gentleman called Boisi Rex. Poor Pip, how she endured those times I shall never know. One day José Luis presented me with an umbrella decorated with a gold band, on which was printed my name. It was an old-fashioned umbrella with a pencil in the head and I had no difficulty in recognising my father's brolly which I still use to this day. Eventually Pip managed to get a divorce and settled with the children in France somewhere behind Cannes where she gambled, always in the belief that El Dorado was around the corner. Later she moved to a houseboat on the Thames when the children were grown up and away. I visited her there once and the only other inhabitant seemed to be a black dancer appearing at the Palladium. Later on still, Pip went to America to make her fortune and bought some property in California. She married again, to a young man called Ian Hanson who worked in cabaret and was some thirty years or more younger than her. Sadly Pip developed cancer out in America and some friends rang me to say she was penniless and ought to be in hospital. We were able to arrange for this and learnt the lesson that one can't be ill in the USA, unless you are insured to the hilt, and of course, Pip wasn't.

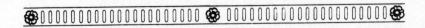

CHAPTER NINE

The Perils of Business

MY FATHER ONCE HAD A FINANCIAL ADVISER, a Hungarian Jew called Dr Fischer. This worthy gentleman had apparently managed to get as far as the beaches of Gallipoli, where my father was fighting at the time, so as to obtain a signature. Dr Fischer had foreseen the great economic debacle in the United States and decided that here was a wonderful opportunity to make money. The idea was to wait until the common stocks had really fallen low and then to buy and wait for the inevitable upturn. The theory was correct and the great collapse arrived. What the doctor had not foreseen was the immensity of the fall. When the stocks fell, say from 200 to 50, he leapt in to buy, only to find that the price was down to 10 or less next week. In the autumn of 1935, it was arranged that I go with my father, and cousin Buster Powles who was over from Kenya, to New York to discuss the situation with the bankers and stockbrokers over there.

Leaving Nucci and our new daughter, a slightly unpopular move, we set sail on the *Aquitania*. The first evening in New York was one that I cannot forget. A kind friend had arranged for Buster and I to attend the heavyweight boxing fight between Max Baer and Joe Louis for the World Championship at the Yankee Stadium. We were whisked off almost straight from the ship and found ourselves in a sea of black people, who had come to root for Joe Louis. There were, however, two quite nice-looking white girls sitting beside us and in an endeavour to be polite, I gently asked, 'Who are you supporting?' to which came a very astute answer, 'We're impartial and I guess if you look around you would be impartial too.' It is history now that Louis won easily and the ride back through a celebrating Harlem was certainly a good beginning to my introduction to the United States. In those days one took one's girl to Harlem in the evening to dance and listen to the strains of a certain Duke Ellington and then walked back in the early dawn through Central Park as the sun picked out the tops of the skyscrapers in the autumn mists. We stayed at the Plaza where Eddie Duchin was playing in the Persian room and Eloise had not yet skibbled down those stairs. Alas, those days are no more.

Our first visit to the Trust company was very enlightening. Very solemn men told my father how much he had lost, at which he smiled and laughed. It was not until quite some time later that I found out that someone had quickly left the room to enquire whether the English Lord was quite right in the head, or merely very eccentric. He could not bring himself to see that losing large sums of money was a tragedy, except for those who could not afford it. Having discovered that Buster lived in Kenya, the President of the Trust company said to him at lunch, 'How very interesting, East Africa, well well, but I guess you get back to the old country for Ascot?' Isolationism was truly in evidence.

Back in the Munich days, my father-in-law had been very taken with an American girl, who came over to study art in Germany. Her name was Parmenia Miguel. He did a bust of her very striking head. Her father was a New York Jew and her mother an aristocratic Chilean lady, a strange mixture, compounded when Parmenia later on married an American Swede by the name of Ekstrom. Parmenia was, in fact, the only person in New York whom I'd already met at that time. In fear and trepidation I rang her and, in that amazingly generous way New Yorkers all seemed to have, Parmenia gave a party for me and I was launched for a most enjoyable stay. I don't remember a great deal about the later parties we attended, except finding myself one evening with Joan Crawford and her then husband, Franchot Tone, with some other friends in a night club. While I was dancing with Joan Crawford I naturally took note of everything I could about her so as to amuse Nucci later. When I wrote back home I remember saying that, of course she was past her best and her neck was not quite what it ought to be. It's amusing to think that I was 22 and Joan Crawford was probably about 27 or 28 with another thirty or forty years of stardom ahead of her.

My sister Priscilla had come over to New York at this time, where she had a friend called Peggy Wagner, whose father was a banker. I was asked to some very smart club by Mr Wagner and found myself sitting next to a venerable man, when the conversation turned to horses. I asked my neighbour if he was interested and the silence that followed was appalling. He, however, laughed and said, 'Yes, I guess so', and that is how I met Mr William Woodward, owner of several Kentucky Derby winners and at that time the best-known owner in the United States.

Many years later, I perpetrated another faux pas, perhaps the worst of my life, when I was having lunch with Mrs Wagner. It was during the war and the big story at the time was the murder of Sir Harry Oakes in Nassau in the Bahamas. Everybody was gossiping about it and all had their own ideas and theories. I arrived when all the party were sitting down to lunch and, for some reason I can't recall, they were all ladies. I started chatting away to my neighbour and airing my views about the murderer's identity. I noticed Theo Wagner looking very alarmed at the head of the table, but I couldn't stop and when I eventually ground to a halt the lady turned to me and said, 'How very interesting – that's my husband.' Looking back I have a shrewd suspicion I was right, but it is still to this day an unsolved mystery.

My father and I went to Canada to see our lawyers, but I remember very little of that trip, except the amazing feat of playing golf on a very wooded course and losing a ball and a club with the same stoke. The ball sliced into the forest on my right and the club slipped out of my wet fingers and got lost in the top of high timber on my left. On the return journey I did rather better at table tennis, when I managed to beat Kay Stammers. She was a member of the Ladies' Whiteman Cup team and had been a finalist at Wimbledon that year.

We returned to New York where Priscilla had been asked to pay the bill at the Plaza and naturally said that her father would pay when he got back. She was greeted with a laconic, 'Okay, I guess the Lord will provide!' Dr Fischer died quite shortly afterwards from what my father called 'dollaritis', that is to say the continual study of the exchange rates. His widow, who had led a rather sad and restricted life in Hampstead, ran away with a band leader in Bournemouth and, I sincerely hope, lived happily ever after.

It was in 1936 that my father made a decision that was to influence my life enormously: to go into the shipping business. This is something I have touched on earlier. He had always had a very keen interest in ships. In his early days he had taught himself navigation on a trip to South America. He had been a pioneer with racing motor boats and when he competed in the Olympic Games of 1908, his only opponent was the famous Duke of Westminster, known as Bendor. On one occasion they actually finished the race together in the same boat. The Duke had invested in a new form of clothing which was supposed to keep out all cold and wet and, as they raced away from the South coast to Calais and back, the Duke's boat was partly upset and he was thrown out. These boats were very long and narrow and probably overpowered for their size and dimensions. My father looked around and saw two large legs protruding from the sea. The unfortunate Duke was rescued before worse befell and no doubt had a lot to say about the balance of his new survival suit.

Later my father used to spend a lot of time with model boats of all kinds on the lake at Chirk. It is, therefore, perhaps not surprising that he should have been persuaded to take an interest in a shipping venture. Exactly how it came about I am unsure, but he decided to go into partnership and put up money to acquire a firm which was called the B & S Company. B was the initial of George Bailey whose main interest was in his repair and dock business. The 'S' stood for Street. Dick Street was a young man, then about 30, and had shown that he had ability and ambition. His father had been in charge of the docks at Cardiff and his brothers, Malcolm and Charles, were also interested in the sea.

It was, in fact, a very good time to go into shipping and I imagine that Dick put forward very strongly and clearly the advantages of the new Scrap and Build Scheme. Strangely enough not everybody was enthusiastic about this at the time, but the Government of the day clearly realised that it could not allow the Merchant Navy to decline in either size or quality, when there was the possibility of war, even if not really believed in. The idea was that anybody who agreed to scrap their old ship received enormous monetary advantage in building a new one. In other words, the shipping world was encouraged to expand and swap old for new.

After a short period the B & S Company was incorporated in a new company known as the South American Saint Line, with the intention of forming a Line, that is to say regular sailings from the Continent, mostly Hamburg and Antwerp, to Brazil, Uruguay and the Argentine; and a return service to London, and later on to Hull. To achieve this position needed immense energy and skill. As in many another trade, the shipping business was controlled by conference; that is to say a conglomeration of companies of all nationalities who control the sailings. To be outside such a conference and in competition was to take on, in our case, not only such British lines as The Royal Mail and the Blue Star but also the big German,

French, Scandinavian, Dutch and Belgian Lines interested in trading in that part of the world. Suffice it to say that we achieved our objective, and in later years, after the War, Dick Street was to become Chairman of that conference. It seems almost incredible to remember that the first ship we built only cost about £100,000. She was probably about 8000 tons and I can remember the trepidation around the board room table when it was suggested that we continue with another at £150,000.

It was not until after the War that I really took a very active interest in the company and became joint Managing Director and later Chairman. At some period in the early days George Bailey decided he must part company with us. However, his son worked in our office and there was no real break in the old friendships. The whole business of setting up a Line, rather than just running tramp steamers, entails having agents in every port, who not only get the cargo for the ships, but advise their sailings and help in any way towards the success of the enterprise. The idea of a conference is, of course, partly to ensure that the same charges are made to all exporters and that there is no undercutting. This objective was somewhat ideal, but it was better than a free-for-all which would have reduced everybody to penury. Before the War, agreements between the Lines were done in gold and it still sticks in my gullet that when war broke out the great German Hamburg Sud American Line owed us some £25,000 in gold, a debt that has never been repaid. When we first joined the conference, the meetings were held either in Paris or London. It is fairly accepted now that these things have a habit of getting increasingly grand. I think it was Dick Street who first suggested that the meeting should be in Torquay for a change. Actually this was rather a success, though I believe that in later years they even ventured, no doubt at vast expense, to Rio de Janeiro. In Paris the conference was held at the George V Hotel and in the evenings we used to go to the Lido or other night spots as the fancy took us. I regret to say that Nucci used to complain that I came back smelling of cheap scent, although I behaved impeccably.

The Germans were the most powerful and the Dutch were very efficient and competitive. After the War I found myself in Hamburg, which had been more or less destroyed. I heard that the representative of the Hamburg Sud was in a bad way and living in a cellar. I bought some coffee and eventually tracked him down in a dismal place. When I gave him the coffee he immediately called his son and told him in German to go and sell it on the black market. As I understood German I was a little hurt, but said nothing: a few years later he was Chairman of the conference and telling us what to do.

Our affairs were looked after at this time by a Mr Cheer. The office was in Windsor House, Victoria Street, although the London estate was run from Queen Anne Street. It was thought sensible to bring everybody together and Queen Anne Street was rebuilt for this purpose in the 1930s. I spent quite a time trying to learn what everything was about. I dearly regret that I had no proper training and I am sure that if I had, some of the disasters that befell might have been avoided. As everyone, with the exception of Dick Street, was a lot older than myself, my father suggested that I find a friend and bring him in to go on the Board and work full time for us. This I did in the shape of Tom Harcourt-Powell. Tom had worked in Germany, spoke the language and had also married a German lady. All seemed set fair but sadly it was not to be. With hindsight one can see where it went wrong and the obvious mistakes and dangers that were lurking in my path. Dick Street thought it would be a good idea to have Ernest Cheer on the Board of the shipping company because of the close financial association with our affairs and Ernest Cheer, in turn, was obviously much impressed by Dick's ability and asked for him on the London Board of the Estate. Without wishing to impugn either of these gentlemen, who are both dead, it later became obvious that, possibly unconsciously, there would be a 'don't ask too many difficult questions and I'll do the same for you' approach. The temptations inherent in an enterprise like shipping were enormous – food, furniture, flats in London, etc. Tom should, of course, have had enough knowledge to spot these things, but sadly he was keen on boating himself and I fear he joined in the general 'how much can I get out of this?' too.

As time went on nothing very seriously wrong happened, but there was no outside experience to say, for instance, after the Suez or Korean boom, 'Shouldn't we be thinking of making a profit on our shipping, maybe going public and keeping control?' Everybody was too entrenched and comfortable and I was too ignorant. I did feel uneasy at intervals and, much to everyone's horror, I asked a well-known merchant bank to go and give a report on the management of the South American Saint Line. This they did and their answer was that its running was very good indeed. I now know better than to rely on experts.

Some years later Nucci and I were travelling in Rhodesia and we both had a gut feeling that things were not as they should be. We ran into a small and rather aggressive Australian called Keith Hogan and persuaded him to come and help me, in particular to see what was going on. Of course bringing him in, unknown and clearly tough, caused a lot of trouble, but I did it all the same. Keith said to me, 'Don't put me on any Boards but let me attend the meetings and I will tell you what I think.' Despite being colour-blind, Keith had served in the Australian Navy. I think he had some sort of management job with Wankie Colliery in Rhodesia and had eventually come to England where he was a director of Powell Duffryn.

After the first meeting of the shipping company he came to me and said very sadly, 'I fear you are being badly cheated and if you go on like this, you will probably have to sell part of the London Estate to bail yourself out.' He drafted letters for me to write to the various people, asking specific questions. This was horrible for me as Dick was a personal friend and we had shared many happy moments together. This was the beginning of the end and Dick died shortly afterwards. I had to break up the whole business and fire everybody. The London Estate was not quite so bad, but if you had just one person running it and deciding on the leases, with no-one else to question it, it was possible for that person to take somebody out to lunch, settle a deal and report back that he had agreed to, say, £10,000 when the proper price should have been £100,000. I don't wish to dwell on this horrible experience except to say that similar things had been going on in Scotland.

In Scotland, apart from Dean Castle and the policies, we owned about 8000 acres stretching a little to the north of Kilmarnock and right down towards Prestwick and Ayr. They were all smallish dairy farms producing milk for Glasgow. I remember when I was fairly young going round some farms with my father and him saying to me, 'You will be offered a dram of whisky at each place and you can't refuse, but I suggest you ask for some of their delicious milk as well, otherwise you will be very drunk.' Very nice people most of them were and, as they could pass on their tenancies to more or less anybody they chose, the house and place was, to all intents and purposes, theirs. It was interesting to see that nearly all the money they spent on their houses went towards terribly smart bathrooms. They were always pleading poverty and asking the landlord to reduce their rents. However, when one of them died he quite often left sums in the region of £50,000 – £100,000!

After the debacle of the Saint Line we still had a connection with shipping. In about 1951 we had bought a firm called Parry, Leon and Hayhoe who were based in South Africa and were involved in ships' agencies, stevedoring, warehousing, travel and insurance. Their offices stretched from Beira in

Mozambique, all round the coast to Walvis Bay in Namibia. The two partners in the business were Mr Leon, who looked after the financial side and lived and operated in Johannesburg, and Mr Hayhoe, a very personable man who travelled a lot visiting the various shipping lines they represented and looking for more business in Europe. It was a very competitive business and our rivals were always stealing our managers and vice versa. When we first acquired the business Nucci and I, together with Charles Street who had left the Saint Line to come out and take over the new venture, visited all the offices starting with Beira and moving to Capetown and Johannesburg. It was most enjoyable and at cocktail parties we met all the staff in each port and the managers and their wives, which gave us some idea of how the whole thing worked.

We had never met Percy Leon and so it was with eager anticipation that we went to lunch with him in Johannesburg. He had a nice house where he cultivated cacti or rather succulents which, I think, is the right term. I remember two things about that lunch – the first was that opposite me on the wall was a very modern picture and the more I looked at it, the more sure I was that it was hung upside down. Very bravely I suggested that this was so and was ultimately proved right. Whether that helped or not, I don't know but we always got on well. The second thing was that when we were served with a supposedly good claret, it was in fact a very inferior bottle of port; I kept my mouth shut about that.

As if to presage the problems to come, when we became the owners of this company the gentleman in charge of the insurance division committed suicide and then the head of the travel division was sent to prison. These two men had been involved in various swindles which, it turned out, had cost the company a great deal of money. The travel man apparently never took a holiday and so his fiddling of the books escaped detection; that is, until we made holidays compulsory. From then onwards there was hardly ever a dull moment. I had realised that there were going to be various clashes of interest on the shipping front. For example, in South America we were in competition with the Blue Star Company, which belonged to the Vestey family, and in South Africa we were their agents – certainly in Capetown. I had no illusions that this state of affairs was likely to last very long. So when a representative of Blue Star, a Mr Trott, arrived in Capetown, Charles Street and I thought it would be a good idea to ask him to dinner at the Mount Nelson Hotel. After dinner, when Mr Trott was about to leave and was climbing into his car, he said to me, 'Oh, incidentally, we are opening our own office tomorrow and Mr So-and-so, your manager, will be joining us. Thank you for a good dinner.' Tough bunch.

The travel business also had its problems. (Indeed, I have been involved in travel several times since, with no great success.) We were probably the biggest travel agents in South Africa, but did not prosper as we were run in the old-fashioned way; that is, having a large office staffed with masses of people who spent most of their time helping old ladies with their train times. There was a small firm called Musgrove & Watson which consisted virtually of these two gentlemen, an office with a mass of telephones and a very small staff. They would then approach a big outfit such as Anglo-American and offer to do all their travel arrangements. The next move was to install one man in Anglo's office so they could deal directly with him. This turned out to be a great success and they flourished. When we got desperate with our antiquated travel business, we negotiated and eventually bought Musgrove and Watson. Tiny Musgrove ran all our travel and eventually became the manager of the whole of Parry, Leon and Hayhoe: a most charming man who has only just died as I write. We became very good friends and had a lot of fun together.

A few years later Tiny Musgrove was instrumental in our

making a first visit to Australia. Nucci and I had taken our youngest daughter Millie and another Camilla, daughter of Kenneth Keith (now Lord Keith), on a visit to Kenya and then on down to South Africa. We didn't quite know what we were going to do next. Tiny Musgrove reminded me that we were agents for the Cunard Line and their famous cruise ship, the *Caronia*, was due shortly in Durban on the way to Australia. 'Why don't you go and see Australia?' So we did. Like a lot of other people I had always thought of it as 'that desert on the other side of the world where they play cricket'. The *Caronia* was mostly filled with old people, Americans, on a long world cruise. Our two young girls of 17 (Camilla Keith was going through the phase of having to have everything 'flambée') amused themselves with the younger ship's officers on the comparatively short trip to Freemantle and Perth.

We were only in Sydney for five days and then returned home via Hong Kong and Bangkok. Despite our short stay, Nucci and I were rather taken with Australia and we began to think of some kind of investment in the country. Keith Hogan suggested as a plan of campaign that he and Ronald Leinster, who was also with Howard de Walden Estates, should go out there and talk to various people while Nucci and I should try and stay with some of the State Governors so we could check any ideas with them. It was at first presumed that the investment would be agricultural, as we had just given up the farming interests in Kenya. On our next visit Nucci and I were fortunate to stay with General Sir Douglas and Lady Nora Kendrew in Perth; we became friends and stayed several times in later years. We then stayed with the Governor-General, Dick Casey, and his wife Maie in Canberra and I learnt what little I know about Australian art from Maie, who went on flying her own aeroplane until well into her eighties. Finally we stayed with General Sir Rowan and Lady Joyce Delacombe in Melbourne, who became great friends and still are to this day. Our stay coincided with the Melbourne Cup. There seemed to be several parties and dances every night and it was then that we got to know lots of people, including Sir Jock and Lady Marjorie Pagan. One evening Jock and I got back to Government House at about 2 a.m. and he said we ought to go to the so-and-sos, as it would be good fun. But there was no car, until Jock spotted a huge one belonging to the American Ambassador. We decided to risk it and purloined the giant beast. Nobody seemed to mind and the next morning the ambassador was very affable. In 1967, when I was Senior Steward, I was asked to give a speech at the Horse of the Year dinner given by the Victoria Racing Club at Flemington racecourse near Melbourne. Then they very kindly made me a life member of the V.R.C., which I treasure greatly. Now that I have one or two racehorses out there I hope I shall be able to enjoy this hospitality once again.

Back in Sydney Nucci and I went to stay with Jim and Irene Ashton out near Cowra, about one hour's flight from the city. Late one evening I was discussing Teilhard de Chardin with their daughter Rosie and I remember thinking, 'this is not the Australia I expected.' (Rose became a leading politician in the New South Wales Parliament and is now happily married.) Although we thought seriously about an agricultural investment, we came down in favour of a property investment in Sydney and went into partnership with Sir Paul Strasser. Sadly he is now dead but his widow Vera still lives in Sydney. There is a nice story of their earlier days. As Hungarian Jews they managed to make their escape to America and he started a business in California. One day Vera is supposed to have said, 'This isn't far enough', and they moved on to Australia where he made a fortune.

We eventually sold out of Walden Properties, as the partnership was called, and now we have no financial interest in Australia. I did buy a small property called Coolaroo, near Bowral and Mittagong, which I later sold simply because we didn't go there often enough although it was a lovely place and had a glorious garden. I have never been able to persuade my children or grandchildren about the future of Australia. I am sure they are wrong and I think I could live there quite happily. As a young person, I can't believe that, given a good job, there is any nicer place to have one's home than Sydney.

CHAPTER TEN

War and South America

M
Y ARMY CAREER WAS LITTLE DIFFERENT from that of thousands of fellow officers, so I merely single out two episodes which perhaps illustrate the oddities and sillinesses that crop up in times of war.

In 1941, we were stationed in Duncombe Park, just outside Helmsley in Yorkshire, and were endeavouring to become trained as an Armoured Regiment. One day I was told by my Commanding Officer that the Brigadier wanted to see me and that he also would be present. I had no idea what it was about and was surprised when the Brigadier said to me, 'you have been selected out of the whole of the Division to go to the Staff College'. As I was not a regular soldier I really couldn't have cared less. He continued, 'However, I am afraid I cannot agree to this appointment as your wife has Nazi connections.' I managed not to say anything stupid, which was particularly hard as I knew that at that moment Nucci was entertaining the Churchills at Chirk! I simply said that I couldn't, and wouldn't, accept the remark and he must either withdraw it or I must ask for an interview with the General. That evening I rang my Father and asked him to verify with the War Office that they had nothing against Nucci or me, and of course they hadn't.

The long and short of it was that I went to the Staff College, but more amazing was that when Winston Churchill heard the story he gave Nucci a private number that would find him should any similar emergency arise. Naturally we never used it, but I think it was very admirable of him to show his magnanimity and greatness of character in this way in the middle of a war.

Later in the war I found myself an instructor at the Canadian Staff College at Kingston, Ontario. This was my only appointment about which I protested. If one survived one automatically got the coveted initials P.S.C. with a little dagger that was the equivalent of having been to and passed out of the Staff College in peace time. Any regular soldier would have benefited from this, but as a complete amateur it was of no value to me in any future career. Also, a year away in Canada seemed an eternity, and an extremely cold one too. However, nobody was shooting at me so I suppose I should have accepted with good grace. It was an interesting experience as there was only one other Britisher, a regular gunner, with whom I shared a flat.

It was the custom during the short break between courses, to be seconded to the Canadian Army and despatched to such gorgeous places as Hudson Bay. I found a friend in Washington D.C. who was prepared to get me attached to the American Army so I could go on their manoeuvres in Tennessee, which was a far more attractive idea all round. On this particular occasion he and I were sent to join a certain division somewhere near Nashville. I can well remember waking up in the train and looking out to see that we were actually in Chattanooga in a Choo Choo. The manoeuvres were not particularly exciting and I was treated very deferentially by the General and his staff. Whenever he gave his orders he used to end up saying, 'Now I shall ask Colonel Scott Ellis to give those same orders as it would have been done in the British Army.' At first this was a bit disconcerting, but I rather enjoyed showing that our method was simpler and, in my very humble opinion, a great deal clearer and to the point. After a week or two I suddenly became aware that I had to be back at Kingston in about three or four days, yet here we were wandering about in the Southern States of the USA. I went to see the General, explained my predicament and asked if it was at all possible to borrow one of the small planes that was attached to the Division, as I felt that if I could fly to say Louisville, it should not be too difficult to get a train to Washington and move on from there. To my surprise the General said, 'Go up to the field and help yourself, somebody will fly you there.'

The field was empty of people but there were several planes about. I put my head into a hut and said, 'Would anybody like to fly me to Louisville?' To my mild horror a slightly inebriated sergeant said he would do so. We climbed into a tiny plane and I sat on my suitcase immediately behind the pilot; the whole machine seemed to be made of papier mâché, which it probably was. We took off and I asked the pilot if he had a map. 'Nope', came the reply, so I asked if he had ever been to Louisville. Once again, 'Nope'. I was not very happy, especially as I soon found out that my pilot's idea of flying over the Kentucky Hills, or whatever they were, consisted of following a railway line and occasionally coming down to circle at about twenty feet so as to read the names of the stations. I was beginning to think that my end was near when I sighted a racetrack which I recognised as almost certainly Churchill Downs outside Louisville; then I saw an airfield and told my maniac to land there. It was not a very wise decision either on his part or mine; on closer inspection I saw the field was crammed full of Liberators all painted in RAF colours. However, we landed and I stepped out with my suitcase and a certain amount of thankfulness. My friend immediately accelerated and took off, leaving me in a British uniform holding a suitcase in the middle of a very secret and guarded airfield. It took about one minute before I was arrested and I got no great response by saying, 'I came in that little plane that you can still just see.'

After some time, and with the help of a charming redhead, I managed to talk myself out of this predicament and caught a train to Washington. I began to think of what to do when I reached Washington, as I knew only one person and really had to be in Montreal as soon as possible. On arrival about 6 pm, I rang my friend who said he was in the middle of giving a party but to come round and join in. This I did with some alacrity. After about an hour someone came and said I was wanted on the phone and that it was a lady. Now this was, of course, quite impossible; there was no way anyone could have known I was in Washington unless my host had rung up and told this lady and he said no, he hadn't. So, with a certain amount of suspicion and amusement I lifted the phone. She said, with an American accent, 'Is that John?' to which I obviously said yes. 'Will you take me to dinner tonight?' Thinking the whole thing to be a joke, I said, 'Of course, but who are you and where do we meet?' To which she said, 'Never mind, come to the Statler Hotel at about 8.00 pm and walk round the lobby and I will see you.'

Being young and foolish, I went to the hotel and did as I was told. At the back of my mind was the idea that I would see someone I knew, but to my amazement a very pretty girl, whom I had never seen in my life before, came up to me and said, 'Hello John, shall we go to the Sheraton?' I remember thinking to myself that two can play this game: if she is going to go on pretending, I am not going to ask, and let's see what happens. All I can say is that we had a good dinner and danced and spent the night together and neither of us ever asked a question at all. We both left the next morning and to this day I don't know who she was, why she rang, how she knew me or what it was all about. I got back to Kingston, maybe not too versed in the way of the American army but slightly more aware of the ways of the world.

In 1946, after I had been demobbed, we had planned to go on a trip to South America to pick up the pieces of the South American Saint Line and meet all the Agents and Shippers. It was thought that we should sail in September, but things did not work out exactly as planned. Firstly, we were moving into our new home in Surrey at Wonham Manor, Betchworth. Secondly, Nucci was pregnant and expecting next April. Thirdly, my father was taken ill, but it was not realised by any of us, and I hope not by him, how serious it was. The result was that I set off with Dick Street and some of his family, leaving Nucci to cope with moving in and to do the very little decoration that was permitted in those days. When we were about half-way between Las Palmas and Rio de Janeiro my father died. It transpired he had raging cancer, but he was lucky in that he had no pain and the end was quick and sudden. Of the numerous obituaries written about him there was one that certainly would have amused him. It appeared in a French publication and ended, after referring to his being the landlord of Harley Street, etc, by saying, 'even his own tenants couldn't save his life.'

I realised how futile it was to plan anything and felt there was nothing I could do back in England. It was before regular air flights and so there was no way of getting home quickly, when we did arrive in Rio in about a week's time. I, therefore, decided that the sensible thing to do was to carry on with the business arrangements and get a faster ship home from Buenos Aires when we had finished down there. The result of these decisions was impossible to gauge at the time, but they caused a considerable amount of trouble with the family in the future. My mother gave away things which she had no right to do, and I was not there to help Nucci at a very difficult period. I spent some of the day on which my father was buried in Scotland giving a big dinner at the Copacabana. Such are the vagaries of fate. One good thing, as far as I was concerned, was that the changing of my name occurred in Brazil where I had never been before and, therefore, that transition was over by the time I got home.

When we eventually reached Buenos Aires, having visited Sao Paolo, Santos and Montevideo, I made arrangements to return on a Royal Mail ship that was due to sail direct to England. This was a memorable voyage. The ship had accommodation for about thirty passengers, but I was the only one on that particular trip. I had a steward who looked after me and I wondered how on earth I was going to pass the time. (Incidentally, the next time I saw this steward, he was leading in a winner at Hurst Park!) On the first day at sea he announced that the Captain sent his compliments and would I visit him in his cabin at mid-day. This ritual took place every day. The Captain drank vast quantities of gin and conversed on every subject under the sun. He was a very large man and only wore a singlet. I was puzzled by his conversation as quite often, when launched into some subject such as dreams or whodunnits, he would suddenly stop short and start on something else, as if he had exhausted his knowledge of the first topic. One day I was left alone in his cabin for a short time and for some reason I looked under his bed. There were stacked past copies of *Readers Digest*. The penny dropped: our Captain had a very good memory and had only read that publication. In other words he had read nothing but potted stories and articles and never ever had he been able to follow up one of these. The Chief Engineer, on the other hand, bred exotic tropical fish down in the bowels of the engine room. He was also a very civilised character with whom I spent many hours. Otherwise, I read and walked the decks in solitude for about eighteen days.

To my mild horror our ship was suddenly ordered to divert to Gibraltar and the Mediterranean. This sort of thing was not uncommon in those days just after the War. There was no alternative but to arrange to disembark at Gibraltar and get myself back overland. I had virtually no money and a passport with the wrong name in it, neither of which helped very much. Before arriving in Gibraltar, we called in at Las Palmas on Christmas Eve and there ensued a ridiculous argument between the agents of the Royal Mail Line and our own agents,

Elder Dempsters, as to who should entertain me that evening. At Gibraltar I thought It would be best to try and get to my godmother Princess Bea and her husband Prince Ali at San Lucar de Bairameda. This I managed and they helped me get a train through to Irun and Hendaye, and gave me sufficient pesetas. Now this is where things began to go badly wrong.

When we reached Irun, which is at the border, we were all ordered out of the train with our baggage and a Customs man asked me what money I had. Very foolishly I showed him my bundle of pesetas which he seized and refused to return. I then compounded my stupidity and was lucky to get away with it. I was standing holding my suitcase and there were a number of police around with guns, but I was so angry that I dodged under the barrier and ran across the bridge where I could just see some French officials on the other side. There was a lot of shouting, but fortunately nobody fired, and I arrived in a heap in the arms of a French Customs man who was as stupefied as me, but friendly. I was not to know that England and Spain had broken off diplomatic relations the day before, or that the nearest British Consul resided in Spain, I think at Santander. I was penniless, so what was I to do? I walked to the railway station and found out at what time the next train left for Paris and what was the minimum fare. I then ransacked my suitcase until I came across a small gold bracelet that I had bought for Nucci in Buenos Aires, which I thought I could sell or pawn. Hendaye is probably not much bigger or nicer than it was then, when it afforded me a very uncomfortable afternoon. I tried shops with no success and eventually decided that bars held out a better prospect. My French is not wonderful but it is amazing what desperation will do. Eventually I found a sleazy character who showed a little interest. He thought he had a mug to deal with and he had, but at last I got him to fork out the minimum rail fare and parted with the bracelet. I was so pleased with myself that I didn't mind being cheated and thought my troubles were over. They certainly were not.

When the train appeared I found myself destined to sit up all night on a very uncomfortable wooden bench in a crowded carriage. But I was on my way, though still very innocent about what it is like to be penniless – as I was, of course, once again. When I arrived in Paris, it was still dark and there were very few cars or taxis. I saw a family of three waiting helplessly, so with inspiration I rushed off and found a taxi in the hope that they would offer me a lift. This they did, and politely asked me where I wanted to go. I was tired and unshaven and probably smelt but I said without hesitation, the Ritz Hotel. I can't remember why I gave that address, it was the first one to come into my head. The sequel was at least educational.

I walked in and explained my predicament to the concierge, who couldn't have cared less. I was informed that I could sit in the foyer but could not wash or shave. I asked when the British Embassy opened and was told at 9 o'clock. So I waited and waited and then walked round there. Whoever answered the bell told me that the Embassy was shut as it was New Years Day. I told him I would smash the windows if I couldn't see a duty officer immediately, and that there must be one! There was. I explained my problem and asked for a seat on the Golden Arrow and enough money to get home. He said this was impossible as they only helped totally impecunious Englishmen and I was Lord Howard de Walden. Eventually I persuaded him I really was penniless and then he saw the funny side and was most helpful. I remember I had to sign a paper and give a name of someone in the Foreign Office as guarantor. With what little humour I had left, I entered the Rt. Hon. Ernie Bevin, who was then Foreign Secretary, and whom I had never met and certainly never did, as I would gladly have repaid my debt to him. My duty officer said was there anything else he could do. I asked if he could send a car round to The Ritz to take me to the station and if the chauffeur could call my name out loudly. I returned to the hotel and got shaved, washed and waited for the car. The chauffeur played his part and immediately scores of people rushed up to take my suitcase and help me. With as much hauteur as I could summon, I refused, remarking that my reception on arrival had been rather different and I hoped I wouldn't need their hospitality ever again, So I went off to the station and arrived home that evening when nobody expected me. I didn't really enjoy poverty of that sort, even for twenty-four hours.

The second time I went to South America was in 1948. Nucci and I with Pupa Weikersthein, Ernle Chatfield, together with Charles Street, the general manager, decided that it would be fun to see the famous fiesta in Rio de Janeiro. We travelled on one of our new ships which we built after the war: the *St Thomas and St John*. Nucci had done the decor in the cabins, lounge and dining room. The ship was very comfortable and the food excellent. All I can remember of the outward journey is Nucci and Pupa lying sunning themselves in the really hot sun of the Atlantic. Neither burned and they` became very brown indeed. The fiesta was all and more than we expected. One bought nasty little bottles that squirted ether, which had a very spirited effect when applied to a hot and sticky shirt, but was less amusing if it went in your eyes. It was impossible to sleep, the pounding of the Samba was incessant and one joined in on the streets with everybody else.

We had decided that it would be more sensible and more fun to fly to Sao Paulo as we had to see the agents in Santos. We were due to take off from a small airfield in the centre of Rio at a fairly early hour. It was very hot and I went to wake Nucci and Pupa who had collapsed on their beds the night before. They were both stark naked and fast asleep so I ran two cold baths, and with a little persuasion, got them into the water where they awoke sharply. When we got in the plane it was very foggy and Pupa was fingering her rosary. Someone cheerfully remarked, 'Only fifteen seconds flying time to the Sugar Loaf!' (the little island that looks like a loaf at the harbour entrance). Sao Paulo seemed to contain nothing except banks.

In the afternoon we drove down to Santos and poor Pupa passed out and lay over me all the way. When we arrived, the agents had laid on a cocktail party and a dinner, but Pupa never made either as we couldn't wake her up.

We flew on to Porto Alegre in South Brazil, which is the home of a large colony of Germans whose language is used in all the shops, and then to Montevideo and Buenos Aires where I had quite a lot of business to transact. We eventually set sail for home, and we should have gone straight to Tenerife, but, alas, about the second morning out of Buenos Aires, I sat down in a deckchair and my thumb was in the wrong place when it collapsed. For a second or two I didn't realise what had happened until I saw the top of my left thumb lying by itself nearby. I had the presence of mind to react quickly – I picked it up, stuck it on and held tight: then the pain started. The Captain decided to divert to Rio de Janeiro and called for a doctor to come on board. For two days I held the thumb on, and was given morphia. It was a relief when that beautiful harbour came into view. The doctor gave the thumb one look and said that it had to be operated on. So Nucci, Charles Street and I stepped back into Brazil with no one questioning us.

When I was lying on the operating table, the surgeon approached with a cigarette in his mouth. This was too much and I demanded to have it done with a local anaesthetic and watch what he did. In fact, he did a marvellous job and today, apart from the nail growing crooked, gives no trouble. I had to take penicillin every day and the packets the doctor gave me were the old thick, heavy type. When we got to Tenerife it was suggested that I went to see a doctor to ensure all was well. My thumb was about the size of a tennis ball, but felt all right. The Spanish doctor did a lot of tidying up and then refused any payment because he said he had fought with my sister in the Civil War! This splendid voyage then came to an end with no one ever having spoken a harsh word to another – quite a feat.

CHAPTER ELEVEN

Children and Holidays

A S THE WAR CAME TO AN END NUCCI AND I BEGAN to think about where we were going to live. At that time we were still in a small rented cottage at East Burnham Well near Farnham Common and Farnham Royal. It was necessary to be within striking distance of London as I presumed that I would work there when I left the army. Wonham Manor, Betchworth seemed a suitable place. When we moved in we imported a dear old couple called Wellbeloved who lived quite close. She was supposed to cook and look after the place and he was to help in the garden. It was not a great success, but they stayed for years in a small cottage and were much liked by the children.

We had the three daughters, Hazel and Susie having returned from Canada to join their new sister Jessica. Hazel was nine and in retrospect was the most affected by going to Canada. It is difficult to look back and remember the feelings at the time in parting with two small children. We were begged by the government to do so and yet, looking back, I regret it, especially for Nucci who heard nothing from her family in Germany after Dunkirk either. Poor Hazel seemed to be very troubled and was always crying, sulky and not eating. Our nice local doctor was unable to help and finally suggested that we should take her to see a child psychologist in London. This idea appalled us both, but eventually Nucci took the plunge and I remember she came home not at all amused. The expert said she should give in to Hazel and let her have her own way about everything. Nucci was very determined and bravely decided that she would do exactly the opposite to what she had been told. Hazel soon started getting better and I sincerely hope she does not have any nasty recollections of those sad days.

Susie was more aggressive and used to spit at her mother and anyone else who happened to be about and scream for hours on end. However, she soon became normal and nice. We duly sent them to school at Les Oiseaux near Ramsgate where they seemed to flourish. When it was Jessica's turn to go, she hated it and made the most terrible fuss. We took her away and sent her to the Sacred Heart convent at Woldingham, which was much handier and our fourth daughter Camilla eventually went there also.

Partly because of our shipping interests and thanks to knowing a number of people on the Continent, we were able to take Hazel and Susie to Le Zoute in Belgium in 1946, where they were goggle-eyed at the shop windows full of things they had not seen before. In 1950 all the children, except Camilla, came to Arnbach, which belonged to my brother-in-law, Max Pfetten, about seventy miles north of Munich. We went by ship to Rotterdam and then motored the rest of the way. We went there for the next two years, and to Oberhofen where Nucci had been brought up.

In 1950 Nucci had to have an operation and was in a nursing home in Bentinck Street. I went one afternoon to the Summer Exhibition at the Royal Academy and was very struck by a self-portrait by someone called Pietro Annigoni. I told Nucci I had seen a portrait by someone who really should paint her. I discovered that Annigoni was in London at the time and he agreed to paint Nucci. She gave him a very large number of sittings, but the result was stunning and we were both delighted.

Living near us then was a friend, John Barclay, who was Clerk to the Fishmongers' Company. He asked to borrow Nucci's portrait because he hoped he could persuade the Company to chose Annigoni to paint the Queen. Annigoni did, indeed, get the commission from the Company and painted the outstanding portrait of the Queen, consequently becoming much sought after as a portraitist. I said to him one day jokingly, 'When I am able I would like you to paint me and, as your portrait of Nucci has made you so famous, you can put me in front of the queue of all those Duchesses and so on.'

The chance came in Coronation Year, 1953, when we were 'bringing out' Hazel and stayed in London giving dinner parties and entertaining. In those days the girls had to be chaperoned and seen home, and so on night after night I would be up until all hours then sit for Annigoni at 9.30 each morning. I think it is a very good portrait but I do look rather like a dissipated Florentine, which is what I felt. Annigoni always told me that he didn't really like painting portraits and in his later years his concentration on painting frescoes in Italian churches seems to bear this out. I think he is a great artist and we were lucky he was there at the time.

In the summer of 1953 Hazel went to Scotland for the Perth Balls, etc. All the others, including Camilla who was only six, joined us in Bellagio, a great success, before we drove back via Germany. This became a sort of routine and fitted in well with seeing the family there. The following two years we went to Sirmione and Rimini. The last of these holidays had a very moderate start. We had arranged to go to Riccione where we were told by the travel agents there was a nice hotel. I drove Hazel and Jean Harcourt Powell out via Genoa and Florence. Nucci went by train with two other friends. We arrived after them, but not by much, and as we got nearer, we started to become slightly depressed as the hotel was miles from the sea. We found Nucci sitting on a bed in a nasty little room, saying, 'Disastro!' However, we pulled ourselves together, sent everybody to bed and she and I drove off to Rimini which was not very far, but with no great hopes of finding anything for a party the size of ours at the height of the season. There was one large hotel to the right of the beach which looked like an Edwardian Christmas cake. We pleaded with the management and somehow or other were given rooms in the attic, which didn't worry us at all. As long as we had a reasonable roof over our heads and could enjoy the sea with the children, we would all be happy. We moved in the next day and from then on all went well.

As our ships went to Las Palmas on the way to South America, someone suggested we try the island as our agents over there could help us. So in 1956 we sailed over on the *St Thomas*. It was very rough and Nucci tied Jess and Camilla down in their bunks. I rather wish someone had done the same for me. We stayed at the Santa Catalina Hotel which in those days was about the only one. It had a nice swimming pool and we quite often made excursions to the other end of the island where there was a wonderful beach with no buildings at all, called Mas Palomas. Today Mas Palomas is a vast town and crowded with tourists at all times. Nucci and I began to have ideas about getting a little place on the island and this came to fruition in 1962.

After we had brought out Hazel, we thought that on her 21st birthday or thereabouts, it would be fun to give a party at the Dean Castle to coincide with the Western Meeting at Ayr in September. Hazel asked what friends she liked (which included her future husband, Joseph Czernin) and we asked friends too.

I had been staying at Sledmere, probably for the St Leger, and was about to drive on up to the Dean, when a fellow guest, Kate Smith, said she was going to stay with the Haddingtons at Tyninghame. I suggested I could give her a lift as it was not so very far out of the way. Off we set in my Bentley and we were not far from Kate's destination when disaster struck. We were approaching a left turn with a stone wall on the right and facing us when, I suppose, something went wrong with the steering. To my horror we sailed through the stone wall and I remember well seeing a valley below and thinking, 'What a silly way to be killed.' Very luckily there was a little dead ground and we turned upside down, coming to rest in a ploughed field.

I managed to stop the engine roaring and climbed out through a window. Having discovered that Kate was also intact, I said, 'Come on, quick', and started to try and pull her out by the leg. Her only response was, 'Wait a moment, I can't find my bag!' Kate had a few minor cuts and her clothes were torn; we both looked fairly grim.

We found a cottage where they kindly gave us a cup of tea. I couldn't pick the cup up as my hands were shaking so much but Kate, a lot younger, was able to drink hers. Eventually we got a car to take us on to Tyninghame. How was I going to explain to the Haddingtons, whom I had never met, why I was bringing their guest to them in tatters? Also, what was I going to say to Nucci and Kate's mother, whom I did not know? Lady Haddington could not have been more helpful: we were both put to bed and a doctor sent for to see that no serious harm had been done. None had. I spent a rather nervous evening on the telephone trying to explain where I was and why and that all was well with both of us. The next day I got our factor at the Dean to come and pick me up as I was not up to driving and anyway, the poor Bentley was still upside down in a field. I never saw Kate again, sadly, as she was a lady of spirit; nor the Bentley, nor the kind Lady Haddington. A sad little tale.

By the early 1960s Hazel was married and Susie did not tarry much either. Jessica was 'out' in Scotland and elsewhere. We had only Millie and in 1963 we went with her to Torremolinos. We were to stay at a new hotel called the 'Pez Espada'. I remember Millie looking out of the window at the pool and exclaiming, 'Look, there is Ramon!', and she was right. Ramon had looked after the pool at the Santa Catalina so things were looking up. This was the time we went to the famous *mano a mano* bullfight between Dominquin and his brother-in-law, Ordonez, in Malaga. Millie had already fallen in love with Dominquin who used to come to the pool at our hotel and, indeed, he was a most attractive fellow. The fight itself was remarkable because everything went right. At the end Ernest Hemingway said to me, 'Never go to a fight again. That is perfection and you will never again see anything like it.' I'm sure he was right and I never have. Nineteen sixty-six was the first summer without children and therefore Nucci and I went every year to our villa in Las Palmas, which we named Villa Camilla. Various friends came to stay and we built a swimming pool which was heated. I look back to those days with real nostalgia.

CHAPTER TWELVE

Breeding and Racing

I MUST WRITE SOMETHING ABOUT HORSE RACING, as it has been my major hobby for many years and I have also taken part in its administration. I have related how my interest was first really aroused when I had measles at Snailwell and spent quite a time on the Heath at Newmarket during my convalescence. My father spoke to me about racing very often, probably because I was the only member of the family who was interested. Neither my mother nor any of my sisters took to it at all, just as in later years none of my daughters did either. On many occasions my father talked about Phalaris and how Lord Derby would ruin the breed if he continued to use this sprinter on so many good mares. How wrong he was about that, but sometimes he was much shrewder in his opinions, even if he didn't often take advantage of them. He was a great believer in Blandford because he had a pretty useful animal called Captain Fracasse who was trounced by Blandford on two occasions. Blandford, despite being a cripple, was undoubtedly a very good horse and my father used him early on at Stud, where he, of course, became outstanding.

One day my father decided that I should go and see one of his horses run at Newmarket, a filly called Sundry trained by Dawson Waugh. For some extraordinary reason I was put on a train in the charge of a man called Bob Sievier. He was a real rogue and gambler, who had, however, owned and trained Sceptre to win all the classics except the Derby, so it was certainly a good start to my racing life. Papa always had a soft spot for this gentleman and in later years, he used to buy bull

terriers from him. My father came down to Newmarket later
that day and, when in deep discussion with Dawson Waugh, I
remember overhearing him say, 'We don't want to disappoint
the boy'. Looking back, I imagine the filly was in season, but
they decided to let her take her chance. She was ridden by a
very good young apprentice called Charlie Elliott, who of
course went on to become one of the great jockeys of the age. I
got tremendously excited and shouted and threw my cap in the
air as she won by a short head. Two venerable old gentleman
who were standing behind me patted my head and told me to
be a little bit more restrained. My father said they were Somer-
ville Tattersall and his friend Sir Edward Elgar. Perhaps this
mixing with the mighty gave an extra sparkle to my excitement
but I certainly followed the racing scene as best I could in
future.

By the time I went to Eton I more-or-less knew who had the
best studs and horses and I began to have favourites. For no
particular reason, I found myself always hoping for the success
of Lord Astor and I had immense admiration for all those good
fillies that he had, seemingly year after year: Saucy Sue, Miss
Gadabout, Booklaw and others. There were several of us in the
same class at Eton who were keen on racing. On one occasion
there were sitting at the back of the class: Charles Halifax, Earl
of, who sadly died some years ago, Martin Gilliat, now Sir
Martin, Clive Graham, Bill Curling and myself. We used to
rush out and buy the *Evening Standard* if we had an interest in
any animal running that day. Clive and Bill became respect-
ively 'The Scout' in the *Daily Express* and 'Hotspur' in the
Daily Telegraph.

When I went to Cambridge I had in the next room to me
someone whom I didn't know but who later became a great
friend. Tom Blackwell had no connection with racing and I
introduced him to Newmarket, where to my horror, he took to
betting in a big way. I used to try and persuade him not to have
£100 or more (a huge sum to us in those days) in a selling race

with thirty runners. However, Tom was lucky and when he became an owner he had some very useful horses and built up a very successful small stud near Bury St Edmunds, which his son now owns.

After I married it did not really occur to me to own a horse of my own as my father had his stud and horses and their doings were sufficient for my interest. Nucci and I did not go racing much in those early days, unless there was some particular horse of my father's running somewhere, but I usually went to the Derby and almost always to Royal Ascot. Naturally, during the war, one lost touch as there was little racing and it nearly all took place at Newmarket. When I was at the Staff College at Camberley I had a great argument with someone at lunch as to whether Big Game would win the Derby or not. I thought not and after lunch we went our different ways. When I heard the result, which I forecast correctly, I went to my friend's room to tell him, only to find that he had blown his brains out for no seeming reason, and certainly nothing to do with the Derby.

When my father died in 1946 he had to all intents and purposes given up racing and had sold the Snailwell stud. When I got back home from South America I asked whether there were any horses and was told that if I went to Newmarket and saw Jack Waugh, he might know something. Well he did; he had two or three horses belonging to my father and we decided to continue with them and see what happened. They were in fact all useless, but it was the start of a very happy relationship. It did not take long to decide that if I was going into racing, I had better start from scratch and try and build up a small stud.

I am fortunate in having very simple racing colours – plain apricot. It is generally believed that they must be very old because nearly all the plain colours belong to families who had horses two and three hundred years ago, like the Dukes of Northumberland and Devonshire. But my apricot is only as old as this century. When my Father started racing after he returned from the Boer War, he asked a friend what colour he could suggest to go well with a general background of green. This friend, Augustus John, came up with apricot and I am grateful as it is a very nice colour and easy to see (perhaps too easy for the handicappers sometimes).

Jack Waugh and I went to the Doncaster sales in 1948 with the intention of buying a well-bred yearling filly. Jack, having inspected them all, eventually reduced it to one and told me that Frank Butters and Fred Darling both agreed that this filly by Precipitation out of Sun Helmet was their pick also. When the moment came and she entered the ring, so ignorant was I that when Jack said, 'How high shall I go?' I simply said, 'Buy her', as if I were some modern-day Arab. Luckily things were different then and she was knocked down to us for 8000 guineas, a lot of money but not absurdly expensive. I also bought a cheap colt (later called Jailbird) by Devonian. The filly was called Sanlinea, which was the telegraphic address of our shipping company, the Saint Line, in South America. Sanlinea was a good buy and although she nearly died of colic that first winter, she went on to win good races and was third in the St Leger to Scratch and Vieux Manoir. I bought the odd mare during the next two or three years, and so it all started.

I was elected a member of the Jockey Club in 1952. At the time I knew hardly any of the other members or, for that matter, people in racing generally. I was told to go and steward at Windsor, notorious for there being an enquiry after practically every race. This turned out to be pretty near the mark so I learnt quite a lot. Three years later I was asked to be a Steward of the Jockey Club and of course accepted. At the time I was in fear and trembling of my fellow Stewards, they being Bernard Norfolk, Hugh Sefton and later John Willoughby de Broke, but our work was all a lot easier in those days when there were only about forty members of the Club. We three Stewards used to foregather in the big upstairs room in the Jockey Club at

Newmarket in the morning, if there was a meeting in the evening, and decide what issues would be raised. All the matters that are now dealt with by various committees, including the disciplinary one, were dealt with by us. When I became Senior Steward in 1957 I was extremely nervous and I should think that I am the only member of the Club who has risen to speak for the first time at a meeting, as Senior Steward. I asked Hugh Sefton if he could give me any good advice before my first meeting. He said, 'You will have noticed that Harry Rosebery always gets up at the end of the meeting and asks some question, sometimes very sensible and sometimes quite idiotic. If you are brave enough, you will just say, "no, Lord Rosebery", whatever he asks.' This I did and, and after a stunned silence, the meeting was over. Harry was always very nice to me for the rest of the year.

Hugh Sefton was one of the last eccentrics and a man about whom many stories have been told. I remember him with great pleasure and affection. Hugh was tall and very good-looking and a lot of ladies lost their hearts to him in the hunting field and elsewhere. He was looked upon as very grand and superior and I think people were a little bit frightened of him. I soon discovered that, although he was of an older generation, he was kind and helpful and I like to think that we got on very well. He made a wonderful reply to a young man whom he didn't know, who sat opposite him at lunch at Whites Club. They had a perfectly amiable talk until at the end, the young man said, 'Excuse me, Sir, may I ask what you do?' 'Do?', said Hugh, 'You might as well ask a Hottentot who his tailor is.' John Willoughby de Broke asked him to dinner at John and Rachel's home in London, in Phillimore Gardens, to which Hugh replied, 'How kind. Does the tarmacadam go that far?' In the early days of the war Hugh was sitting with fellow officers in Knightsbridge Barracks where he commanded the Royal Horse Guards. A rather officious man from the War Office had arrived to conduct some business and, thinking he would come and wake these soldiers up, suddenly said, 'Now suppose some German parachutists landed in the park; what would you do?' Hugh crossed his elegant legs and rather wearily replied, 'I think I would send for the military.'

The last story I shall tell about dear Hugh was at my own expense. We were both staying with Wenty and Sarah Allendale at Allenheads for a grouse-shooting week. Hugh was sitting on Sarah's right and I was sitting on her left. Next door to me was a lady whose name I cannot recall, but who asked me if I shot abroad at all. To the best of my ability I regaled her about shooting with Marcel Boussac in France. Marcel Boussac was a very rich textile merchant who had recently acquired the couturier, 'Christian Dior'. Over and above this he was the leading racehorse owner, both in France and England. There was a small silence and Hugh in his grandest manner said, 'Oh John, I like shooting with my pals, but do tell us more about your haberdasher friend.' One could go on but I hope this gives a little flavour of a very respected and kind man who lived in a slightly different age.

It was during my term of office in 1957 that the first international seminar took place, now part and parcel of the racing scene today. The Americans initiated it and suggested that it should coincide with the running of the Laurel Park International race – the brainchild of John Shapiro. There was quite a bit of consternation in the Club when I told them that I thought Bill Weatherby, Clerk to the Club, and I should attend and that the Club should pay our expenses. However, they eventually agreed and off we set. We were met off the plane in New York by Marshall Cassidy who was Bill's opposite number in the New York Jockey Club. It was about 7 am: he was rubbing his hands and said, 'I've just come from a lovely party', and that's what it was like for the next few days. We were taken straight away to see the Aqueduct racetrack and he introduced us to everybody there, as well as at the Jockey Club. We were then flown down to Washington where we were put up in the Mayflower Hotel. The next morning we all met, very formally, Mr George Widener who was the Senior Steward, and faced an audience of racing press and racing people in general. Amongst them I recognised the face of jockey Eddie Arcaro. Mr Widener addressed us and then, to my horror and with no previous warning, said, 'Now Lord Howard de Walden will tell you how television affects racing in the United Kingdom.' Fortunately at that time nobody knew how it affected racing and so I could waffle reasonably happily. Even so, it was a bit of a shock. I was then told I must lead the foreign delegates to meet President Eisenhower in the White House, in the Oval office no less. I made a bad mistake in giving the President a tip for the race in the shape of the Aly Khan's Rose Royale. Needless to say it came nowhere.

In the evening there was a big dinner and ball with an Italian flavour at the Sheraton Hotel. The decor was supposed to capture the spirit of the Palio race in Siena. John Shapiro decided that as Nucci was not with me he would provide a suitable lady companion. Sadly, I can't remember her name, but let us call her 'Bobbie'; a good looking if rather alarming lady. When we sat down to dinner Bobbie was on my right and on her other side was Frankie More O'Ferral, a leading bloodstock agent and a fairly tough, though charming man. Mrs Clare Luce presided and there was a raffle for a really splendid Alfa Romeo motor car. We all had our tickets in front of us under our glasses. When the winning number was read out by Mrs Luce I immediately saw that Frankie had won. So did Bobbie and, without a moment's hesitation, she got up, picked up Frankie's ticket and marched up to claim the car. Frankie was in tears, literally, and I remember going over to Bill Weatherby's table and saying, 'Come and see a sight you won't believe!' However, Frankie didn't take things lying down, soon recovered his poise and went straight up and protested. It was all rather embarrassing as some officials came and asked me if I had seen what happened and I recounted what I had witnessed. Bobbie was carted out of the party and Frankie got his car, which I do not doubt he promptly flogged for many dollars. I can't pretend that I wasn't rather relieved at being single. It was a great party and the next day was the big race day. When we arrived at Laurel Park, John Shapiro told me that the Aly Khan was arriving by helicopter and would I greet him, as he had never met him. It was taken very seriously and I was positioned at the top of a flight of stairs with a gathering of our hosts beside me. The Aly arrived in a scarlet helicopter and started climbing the stairs. I suppose everybody thought it was going to be very formal, but the Aly, on spotting me, rushed up and started off, 'Now, about that foal that you sold me,' which left everyone rather speechless.

Mrs Haines, wife of the eminent New York racehorse owner and breeder, very kindly offered me a lift back to New York after the races in her private plane. I was pleased to accept as I had a cold and felt a bout of flu coming on. I was sitting next to a stranger in the plane and he asked me what I did, so I gave him a short lecture on shipping. When we got out at La Guardia he shook my hand, gave me his name and said, 'I'm the President of the United States Lines.' I retired to bed and kind Mrs Haines rang up to say that she was sending a doctor to see me. As if to explain it she said, 'He is Averell Harriman's brother-in-law.' I felt that I had really reached the top echelons of society in those four days.

I was lucky enough to be able to buy Plantation Stud at Newmarket from John Derby in 1958. I was friendly with Bunty Scrope, who at that time was looking after Lord Derby's studs, and he was well aware that I would dearly love a stud of my own at Newmarket. When John decided to sell Plantation, Bunty let me know and so I had really no opposition. Later on when he retired from working for Lord Derby, Bunty managed my stud, to be followed by Leslie Harrison.

I was not a lucky owner for many years, but looking back to those early days, like so many other things, it seemed much more fun then. My first winner was the Devonian colt, Jail-bird. It was at Chepstow and ridden by Tommy Lowry who beat Gordon Richards by a short head. It was before the advent of the photo finish and I am glad, in retrospect, that it didn't exist. I couldn't have stood the strain. One day Jack Waugh and I agreed that it would be fun to buy a foal to win the Brocklesby Stakes at the opening meeting of the season at Lincoln. It had to be cheap and the whole thing was a sort of joke between us. However, Jack bought a filly afterwards called Vermeil. In 1955 we duly won the Brocklesby at Lincoln and also won twice at Hurst Park. The following year she won again at Lincoln and also at Ascot. She cost 600 guineas, a good buy. In 1955 I also had a filly that I had bred called Malcolmia who had won twice as a two-year-old and also had won the Ellisham Stakes at Epsom, when it was confined to fillies. We were hopeful of a good run in the Ribblesdale Stakes at Royal Ascot, but when that day dawned there was one of those famous Ascot storms and the race was postponed for a long period. After the delay Malcolmia was in a real sweat and didn't do herself any justice in the race. When I got home to Wonham, a horse I had turned out called Struelpeter had been struck by lightning and a little dachshund we had at the time had died of a heart attack in the kitchen. A day of woe.

I suppose Amerigo was the first serious horse I bred. He was a chestnut by Nearco which was supposedly not a good thing. He was outstanding as a foal and excitement was intense when he went into training. Jack thought a lot of him and he made his debut at Hurst Park; this was 1957. On the way down to the start he deposited his jockey Eph Smith on the floor and at the start he never got off and was left at least six lengths. Jack put his glasses down with a smothered expletive. However, all of a sudden Amerigo flew past the field and won easily. I began to have exciting ideas and especially when he won the Coventry at Royal Ascot in a canter, by about six lengths or more. He started a hot favourite at Sandown for the National

Produce Stakes but sulked and only finished third. It is said
that a racehorse needs ability, soundness and a good temperament. Amerigo sadly lacked the latter attribute. Jack tried
everything but eventually I sold him after the next year's Derby
to America where he was a great success. He was also a success
at stud. I think the tight tracks in the USA, always on the bend,
were more conducive to Amerigo than the wide-open spaces of
Newmarket.

Another horse I remember with great affection was Panjan-
drum, for two particular reasons. Geoffrey Freer, who was
then the senior handicapper and a friend, said to me at Royal
Ascot, 'I saw a horse of yours run the other day somewhere
and came to the conclusion that he must be one of the slowest
horses in Europe.' So I was more than delighted when Panjan-
drum won the King George V Stakes at the same Royal Ascot.
I was a steward at Royal Ascot in those days, in fact for
twenty-five years, and one was quite often asked for dinner at
Windsor Castle by Her Majesty the Queen. Apparently there
was a custom that if one of her stewards won a race, she, the
Queen drank their health and they, in turn, had to make a
speech. I had no idea of this but, thank goodness, Hugh Sefton
warned me of my fate. Having started my speech correctly
with 'Your Majesty, Your Royal Highnesses', I rather rashly
continued, 'and all you other Panjandrums', thinking this
rather amusing, only to discover that nobody knew what I was
talking about.

Later on I had a horse called Fool's Mate who was trained
by Henry Cecil. This animal had been hobdayed (an operation) for his wind and gelded as a yearling, so his start was not
auspicious. Fool's Mate made his first appearance at Warwick
and was ridden by a small apprentice called D. Smedley. He
was not fancied in any way and the favourite was a stable
companion owned by Sir Reginald Macdonald Buchanan.
However, to everybody's surprise, and particularly that of Mr
Smedley, Fool's Mate won. Dear Sir Reginald was not very

pleased and I don't blame him, although I was soon forgiven. Fool's Mate won twelve races for me over the years, but the most memorable was in 1976 at Goodwood. Ridden by Lester Piggott, he won the Trundle Stakes, then stayed down by the sea to paddle and came out again on the Saturday in the big PTS Laurels Handicap. He duly won and I drove home with the car full of Waterford glass. On the way I stopped off to have a drink with Pris Hastings at Kingsclere. While we were sitting on the terrace a hot air balloon came down in a wheat field and set the whole thing ablaze.

I don't know whether it is a record, but I had a filly called Stocktaking by Premonition out of Malcolmia: well enough bred to be beaten at Catterick at odds of 20–1 on! One of the things that strangely seems not to work is calling horses after your family or home. I have tried Hasujeca (the first two letters of all my daughters' names: useless beast), Chirk Castle, Coollaroo (a property we owned in Australia), Snailwell, none with any measure of success. I have never been interested in the betting side of racing. I always feel that by the time your horse has got to the start, it has cost a lot; why add more? Perhaps I miss out, but I am almost certainly better off as a consequence.

The day that Noel Murless, later Sir Noel, asked me if I would like to buy a few of the Sassoon mares, was the day that luck touched me. At that time the Sassoon studs were at the top. Sir Victor had recently died and I believe his widow needed to raise a little money. Naturally I replied to Noel, 'What's the catch?' 'Oh none', he said, 'except you will have to buy a stud in Yorkshire.' I didn't want a stud in Yorkshire, but having seen Thornton, near Thirsk, I was captivated by its beauty and so a deal was done. I bought about six Sassoon animals and – here comes the lucky bit – one of them was Soft Angels who had been the best two-year-old of her year and was in foal to Tudor Melody. The foal born was a filly named Dulcet who was quite good, although not top class. I felt sure she would be an admirable brood mare, but when she retired to stud she soon died of grass sickness. Meantime, Soft Angels had another two fillies; the first broke her pelvis and the second was Doubly Sure who was quite useless. It so happened that Soft Angels then refused to breed any more, so I was obliged to keep Doubly Sure to preserve the line. I told my manager, Leslie Harrison, to find a cheap and fast horse to send her to. He came up with Sharpen Up, then standing at £200 down the road. Sharpen Up was to become one of the great stallions. Doubly Sure's first foal was Kris who, as all racing people will know, won fourteen of his sixteen races and became a champion stallion. His full brother Diesis is now making his name as a sire. Such are the romances of racing!

Previous to this I had owned a horse who was definitely good, but had a temperament problem; he was called Oncidium. Eventually he won the Lingfield Derby Trial very easily and started second-favourite for the Derby, in which race he was very disappointing. Jack Waugh suggested that I send him to George Todd at Manton, a complete change of atmosphere from Newmarket. This worked well and I duly won the Coronation Cup the next year. Sadly he was got at before the Gold Cup at Ascot, which he was fully expected to win. George wouldn't believe that anyone could do this, as he employed girls. That they had boyfriends had apparently not occurred to him. George Todd was an extraordinary character and very amusing to train with. He thought Oncidium should run in the Arc de Triomphe in Paris and I was horrified when I read in the papers that Oncidium had failed the starting stall tests there. I managed to get a reprieve and he passed the next morning. There were no stalls in England in those days. George was quite unabashed and said, 'Oh, they use those things there, Oncidium has never seen one.' His whole attitude was summed up in his favourite remark, 'I never travel. I went abroad once to a place called Passchendale, didn't like it, have never been again.' Oncidium became a great success in New Zealand and his progeny won many important races in Australia.

After I had bought Soft Angels and a few others, I had horses in training with Noel Murless, among them Magic Flute. Magic Flute was the best two-year-old filly and was fully expected to win the One Thousand Guineas the next year. However, she was beaten by her stable companion, Altesse Royale. I was very hopeful of winning the Coronation Stakes at Royal Ascot. When the day arrived, Noel was in a great state about the going and said to me, 'I don't know whether to run her or not.' For once I got my own back by replying, 'If she belonged to me I think I'd run her,' and she won by six lengths. Noel was very possessive about which horses ran where and the owner really had little say. After I had won the Ribblesdale Stakes at Ascot with Parmelia, I said I would like to run her in the Yorkshire Oaks. 'Oh no', said Noel, 'that's for Lupe, you can win the Parkhill', and so it turned out. However, I insisted she ran in the Prix Vermeille and she was third, with Lupe nowhere.

In 1973 and 1974 Nucci's health had started to deteriorate and nobody seemed to quite know what it was about. Some ten years or so before this we had moved from Wonham to Ormeley Lodge just outside Richmond Park. The main reasons for moving were the difficulty in getting good staff to keep the place going and the fact that the daily drive to London and back was becoming a distinct grind. Poor Nucci continued with all her staggering energy, but clearly there was something seriously wrong. It transpired that she had some form of leuk-aemia. She had to suffer the dreadful transfusions and seemed to get better, until one day she was sent home from the hospital apparently cured. All went well for a bit and she started all her parcelling for Christmas at which she excelled. One evening she looked at me and we both knew that the other knew that it was the end of the road. She collapsed in our bedroom and never regained consciousness. She died peacefully in her own bed and her sister Cucca was able to come over from Germany to be with her at the end.

All the girls were marvellous and supportive; we were happily married for forty years. My mother died about two weeks earlier so it was a heavy double blow. It was a very kind thing that Connie and Peter Burrell asked me to stay in Lyford Cay in Nassau the next month and I was able to start readjusting in completely new surroundings. It never entered my mind to get married again; after all I was sixty-three at the time, but one never knows what is in store.

When I became Senior Steward for the third time in 1977, I asked Simon Weatherby one day in the Jockey Club offices in Portman Square, to show me a list of all of the people employed there. I happened to see the name Lady Mountgarret. As I did not know the title I asked who she was and was told that she was a friend of Charles Weatherby who did a bit of temporary work for the Jockey Club at intervals. I was introduced to her and thought no more about it until, some time later, I ran into this lady in the corridor and asked her if she was going to York races. She replied that she was but that her car had broken down. I offered her a lift, which was duly accepted and the next day we set off. I was going to stay with the Halifaxs at Garrowby and Gillie was going a bit further to stay with the Storeys at Settrington.

I realised that, what with the traffic and talking too much, we were going to be late at York. I knew that Her Majesty the Queen was going to be at lunch in the Chairman's box and I guessed that I might well be sitting next to her. I remember saying to Gillie, 'We're going to be late and I shall have to think of some excuse.' She asked me what I would say and replied, 'Oh, I'll think of something.' I dropped Gillie off at the course, arranged to meet afterwards and hurried up to the box. As I feared, everybody was seated and there was an empty seat next to Her Majesty. I made my excuses about the traffic as best I could, to which The Queen said, 'Is that the only reason?' I can't imagine what inspired me to reply, 'No, ma'am, I proposed to my lady passenger at Ferrybridge', which of course was absolute nonsense. The Queen smiled and then said, 'What did she say?' I answered that we had decided to wait until we were a little bit older. At least this absurd conversation broke the ice and I fear that Her Majesty must have thought that I was quite mad.

As it so happens we did not waste much time: the York meeting was at the end of August and we were married on 27th October. When you reach that age – 66 – there is no point in hanging about. But it had nothing to do with Ferrybridge. Gillie brought me very good luck with the horses and everything else as well. Kris was followed by Diesis and Slip Anchor – quite a good run in six years. We were married in Newbury and had a lovely service of blessing in our own church at Avington and have lived happily ever after.

Two other very lucky things happened to me, the first, my tiny early entry into National Hunt Racing. I had for some time had a few horses with Ernie Weymes who trained at Middleham. We had our successes, the best of which were when Ernie said he would like to run a horse of mine called Rodado in the Moorland Brewery at Newbury. I rather rudely asked him if he knew the way, but he arrived with a northern jockey called Eccleston and the horse won with some ease. He also won for me The Princess Margaret Stakes at Ascot with Sarissa. Anyway at this time he had a horse of mine that had at last won a small flat race at Edinburgh at the end of his three-year-old career. I thought he ought to be sold and Ernie tried to get £1000 with no success. Eventually, I rang up Fred Winter, who lives quite close to us, and asked him if he would take the horse and see if he jumped. The horse was called Lanzarote who won twenty-six races including The Champion Hurdle and sadly had to be put down when falling in The Gold Cup at Cheltenham, which I always think he should have won. He gave me an enormous amount of fun and, having been quite ignorant about jumping, I learnt a great deal.

Some years later Leslie Harrison and I were talking and we

agreed that it would be interesting to buy a German mare or filly, as they were tough and almost free of Phalaris Nasrullah blood. This was the start of the second very lucky thing that befell me. Leslie went off to see a filly, supposedly the best in Germany, but didn't like her, and on the way back he paid a visit to the famous Schlenderhan Stud owned by Gabi Oppenheim. He liked a mare very much but she was not for sale. A few years later they were prepared to sell her so I became the owner of Sayonara.

The obvious thing was to send her to Mill Reef or Shirley Heights as this exotic cross would show us if our ideas had any value. To Mill Reef she had a filly called Sandy Island, who was good, but the ground was against her in her three-year-old career. Despite this, she won the Pretty Polly and the Lancashire Oaks and was second in the Ribblesdale. To Shirley Heights she bred Slip Anchor. Slip Anchor had some breathing problems as a two-year-old and when he won eventually at Nottingham, the assistant trainer was equipped with oxygen in case he was in trouble after the race. However this passed and the next year he started favourite for The Derby.

It is difficult to recapture the excitement of those heady days. I remember attending all sorts of luncheons and dinners, and at all of them Steve Cauthen, who was to ride him, would come up to me and say, 'Relax, my Lord, we shall win', to which I used to say, 'Stop it. Go and have another ice-cream or something.' The whole build-up is quite a strain and owning the Derby favourite is quite an experience.

In fact, that Derby day started rather ominously for us. We had decided to go to Epsom by helicopter, but when we reached Battersea, the weather was so bad that all the helicopters had been grounded. However, a friend came up to me and said that Sheik Mohammed's helicopter, which is an enormous thing and has all the gadgets that the other helicopters hadn't, was allowed to fly and there were two seats left and would we like to have them. Well, of course we accepted and arrived happily at Epsom only to find that several jockeys, including Steve Cauthen, had also been held up. So there were one or two very anxious moments: firstly when I thought I wasn't going to see the race at all and then thinking that I was going to see the race, but who on earth would be riding him? However, all turned out like a fairy tale. I believe I watched the actual race with very little emotion, except to turn to Gillie, when the horse rounded Tattenham Corner about ten lengths ahead and say, 'Unless he crosses his legs he can't help winning!' He had made every yard of the running and won, pulling up, by seven lengths. Gillie and I drove back to London after the race, and when we got home, spent the evening quietly by ourselves. The parties were to follow.

So, on the whole, after getting on for forty years, I have built up a reasonably successful stud and I have bred, and owned, a Derby winner. I very much hope that I shall do it again.

Epilogue

I THINK THE TIME HAS COME TO STOP. ANY OF MY grandchildren or great-grandchildren who have got this far may expect some advice. They will not get any, as I firmly believe you only learn from your own experience and their lives and circumstances will be quite different from my own. Let them live their lives and I hope they enjoy them as much as I have mine.

One can be allowed a few regrets and these I am happy to admit, for what they are worth. The first is that I never learnt to dance well. Despite hero worshipping Fred Astaire I must have lacked the will or something and so missed out on an enjoyable activity. It is too late to rectify this, but not too late to put right my second regret: I would dearly love to speak fluent Spanish. Spain was always my favourite foreign country and I should have learnt it during my youth. My third regret is that I never learnt to fly. Now that we are fortunate to have a little plane of our own, that hankering still lurks round the corner, but I am too old and would never master the radio side of things, even if I managed the rest. I wish I had been really good at some game, preferably Rugby Football and I would dearly love to have played at Twickenham. I wish I had been trained in business and done a course in accounting.

I must be very lucky if these are my only serious regrets to set against a happy childhood and two very happy marriages; splendid children all with nice families; a lovely home. I remember going to see my father-in-law when he was dying. He called me back as I was leaving and said, 'I have had a lovely life and I am content. I hope you will be able to say the same.' Fortunately I am still alive and healthy, but yes, I am content.